SO-AXJ-168

The Remarkable

JOURNEY *of* JONAH

The Remarkable

JOURNEY *of* JONAH

*A Scholarly, Conservative Study
of His Amazing Record*

HENRY M. MORRIS

First printing: October 2003

Second printing: October 2006

Copyright © 2003 by Henry Morris. All rights reserved. No part of this book may be used or reproduced in any manner whatsoever without written permission of the publisher, except in the case of brief quotations in articles and reviews. For information write: Master Books, Inc., P.O. Box 726, Green Forest, AR 72638.

ISBN-13: 978-0-89051-407-8

ISBN-10: 0-89051-407-0

Library of Congress Number: 2003107713

Illustrations by Ramona Lowe

Printed in the United States of America.

Please visit our website for other great titles:
www.masterbooks.net.

For information regarding author interviews,
please contact the publicity department at (870) 438-5288.

Master
Books

A Division of New Leaf Publishing Group

CONTENTS

FOREWORD

The account of Jonah and the whale stands out as one of the most difficult stories to believe in the Bible. It has been the subject of extensive ridicule, the source of Hollywood caricature, and the brunt of many jokes. Skeptics focus their deepest criticism at the very concept that a man could be swallowed by a whale and live to tell about it. Yet the Lord Jesus Christ believed it to be a historical fact. To Him it was so true that He labeled it as an analogy to His own death and resurrection. If the type isn't true then the essence of Christianity isn't true. As Christians we have no option regarding the historicity of the Cross and the empty tomb. Our entire world view and eternal destiny hang in the balance. Thus, we have no option in believing the story of Jonah.

The two stories are different in at least one very important way. There is much historical evidence attesting to the life of Christ and accuracy of the gospel accounts. Every turn of the archaeologist's spade uncovers more evidence supportive of their truthfulness. Some have even called Christ's resurrection from the dead "the best proved fact of history." The defender of the gospels stands on solid ground.

Jonah's tale, on the other hand, contains comparatively few names and places which can be verified. Most notably, it rests on the existence of a great fish or whale big enough to swallow a man and then the man's disengorgement from that whale, but no such creature is known with certainty. Nor are there external accounts available which verify the claims. Taking place much further back in history than the days of Jesus Christ, we have noticeably fewer artifacts and records on which to rely. It takes careful study and clear reasoning to bring the Book of Jonah to life, and it takes a faith-filled, careful thinker to attempt to expound it.

Into those uncertain waters enters Dr. Henry Morris, my father, author of scores of books in several different fields. By training he is a scientist, whose textbook on hydraulics is in use by engineers across the land. In recent years, he has focused his writing on the relationship of the Bible to science, becoming the foremost proponent of scientific creationism, and "foundation-layer" for today's large and powerful creation movement. His passion, however, is Scripture and seeing unbelievers come to trust its claims and believers strengthened in their faith in its accuracy and application. He has gained a working familiarity with study tools in the original language of the Bible necessary to facilitate his study, and has read extensively in many fields. His popular treatments of Genesis, Psalms, the works of Solomon, and Revelation are loved by thousands, as is his annotated study Bible, *The Defender's Study Bible*.

Someone once accused him of being a "speed reader with a photographic memory," but he denies this. Having been both a son and a colleague, I could also testify that his ability to assimilate that information and integrate it into a biblical/creationist world view is astounding. Surely he has been prepared by God to adequately address this wonderful Book of Jonah.

The biblical book is short, and so is this commentary, but both contain rich insights into the nature of God and His dealings with man. As you read, notice the closely constructed logical arguments, and the winsome defense of opinions not universally shared by expositors. I encourage this because the book is so well written and so engaging you'll find yourself nodding in agreement and exclaiming, "Of course! Now I understand. Why didn't I see it before?"

In closing, I not only recommend this book, I recommend its way of thinking. It comes from the mind of a man uniquely equipped to carry out such a study, and the heart of a man who loves and obeys God, and has spent a lifetime studying His message to mankind.

— John D. Morris

INTRODUCTION AND ACKNOWLEDGMENTS

The story of Jonah is a fascinating tale of adventure that at first seems so incredible that few people take it seriously enough to realize that it is a *true* story. Jonah was a real man, a courageous prophet of God whose body survived three days in the belly of a whale and whose soul and spirit survived those same three days out of the body in sheol (translated "hell" in the Old Testament). Then he returned to his prophetic ministry, preaching so powerfully against the wickedness of the Assyrians in Nineveh that the entire city repented and turned to God.

All this was confirmed by the Lord Jesus Christ, and Jonah has thereby become a striking type of Christ in terms of his willingness to die for others, his descent into hell, and his bodily return to life and ministry. Jonah's record of these real-life adventures is fantastic, and yet is presented in such a matter-of-fact way that it clearly has the ring of truth, even without Christ's testimony.

I have now had the temerity to undertake a verse-by-verse commentary herein on this very succinct little four-chapter Book of Jonah. Although I admittedly have had no formal training in seminary or Bible college, the daily, loving study of the Scriptures has been my privilege for over 60 years, and perhaps this will substitute. I have, of course, read many commentaries, books on apologetics, and other relevant materials as collateral reading, and this may help as well.

In any case, I have undertaken this challenge with delight, writing the commentary in narrative form which, I hope, will help make Jonah and his amazing life more real to readers than they may previously have realized.

Furthermore, Jonah indeed is a beautiful type of Christ (the Lord himself said so!) and his "adventures" can be woven into a wonderful gospel message as well as a missionary challenge.

Finally, since this action is centered in the Middle East, especially in what is now the nation of Iraq, it could even have a very modern parallel if we view it in that light, even though it took place some 27 centuries ago. At least I have found it to be uniquely fascinating and relevant, and hope that any readers will find it so as well.

In writing it, I have profited from the reviews and critiques of my two sons, Dr. Henry Morris III and Dr. John Morris, both of whom are excellent Bible students in their own right. Also, the latter has written a kind foreword, which I certainly appreciate. Another of my children, Mary Smith, has typed and edited the manuscript, and made good suggestions of her own.

A special word of thanks is due Ramona Lowe, who prepared all the illustrations, freely as a labor of love for the Lord and His Word, and for the ICR ministry in general. As will be obvious, she is a wonderfully talented artist and a devoted Christian, and this contribution is specially appreciated.

And now, I hope that you also will find this book interesting and helpful in your own knowledge of the Lord, His Word, and His ways.

ONE

JONAH —
THE MAN AND THE BOOK

The Old Testament Book of Jonah is the story of the almost incredible experiences of one special prophet in ancient Israel. The famous "fish story" of his survival from a three-day incarceration in a whale's belly has been an object of unbelief and ridicule by skeptics for more than 27 centuries now. The same is true to almost the same extent with regard to his subsequent preaching in the great and wicked city of Nineveh in Assyria, resulting in the mass conversion of the entire city to faith in the true God. No extra-biblical record confirming either event has ever been found by historians or archaeologists, and so most scholars have concluded that the entire story is legendary and never really happened.

Practically all liberal religious scholars and theologians have jumped to the same conclusion, developing the pious theory that the author of the book was simply writing an allegory or parable of some kind, with Jonah and his experiences somehow symbolizing the nation of Israel and her travails in the world.

And yet the Lord Jesus Christ — the Creator, Savior, and Judge of the whole world — accepted the entire record of Jonah as absolutely real and profoundly important. For all who believe in the incarnate deity of Christ, therefore, and in the inerrant authority of His written Word, the Holy Scriptures, it is essential to believe and study Jonah's record as a factual history of real significance even today. That is the purpose of the exposition in this little book.

First of all, we must realize that Jonah was a real man and a prophet sent by God, not merely a fictional character in a parable. Although there have been many and varied attempts by scholars to "spiritualize" the record into a non-historical allegory or fable of some kind, all such attempts have been refuted and discredited by conservative writers, so no attention will be devoted herein to such notions.

For those readers interested in dealing with *that* realm of speculation, the small book *The Problem of the Book of Jonah* is recommended as an introduction. It was written by Professor G. Ch. Aalders, who was professor of Old Testament in the Free University of Amsterdam, when his book was published in 1948 by the Tyndale Press of London, as based on a lecture originally delivered in Tyndale House, Cambridge. In that small monograph, Professor Aalders has compellingly refuted all these non-historical views of the Book of Jonah, insisting that the intent of the writer was simply to recount the real factual experiences of Jonah, incredible as they may have seemed.

That motivates this brief commentary as well. Jonah's account is taken at face value, not only as true history but also as a divinely inspired component of the canonical Old Testament Scriptures. That is the way it was taken by the Lord Jesus and by the Jewish scribes and religious authorities of His day, so that should be good enough for us.

The book was originally written in Hebrew, of course, as transmitted by skillful and careful copyists over many generations, compared and standardized eventually by dedicated Masoretic scholars, all prior to the invention of the printing press. There have been numerous English translations in recent years, but the one used herein is the highly accurate and time-tested Authorized King James Version. Due attention is paid to the insights of other translations whenever appropriate.

The Book of Jonah was almost certainly written originally by the prophet himself. It was written in the third person, but this was a common style of writing, even in autobiographical narratives. No one would have been able to write about his unique experiences except Jonah himself. Presumably the accounts were written later, perhaps after his return to Israel from Nineveh, but they were so extraordinary as to be indelibly etched in his memory (not to mention the overriding influence of the Holy Spirit, the ultimate author of all the books of the Bible).

The Book of Jonah, with all its supernatural aspects, was apparently accepted by the Jews as true and authoritative right from the start. It was included as canonical among the books of the prophets, even though (alone among all these books, from Isaiah through Malachi) it contained no prophecies except the one (Jon. 3:4) proclaiming the imminent doom of Nineveh. That prophecy was not fulfilled until much later, of course, because the people of Nineveh did repent at that time.

Jonah did have true prophetic credentials, however. His father was named Amittai (meaning "truthful"), and he had been raised in the town of Gath-hepher, in the region given to the tribe of Zebulon west of the sea of Galilee (see Josh. 19:10, 13), near the present site of Nazareth. This region later became known as Galilee and was in King Herod's tetrarchy during the time of Christ.

Jonah had uttered a famous prophecy which had been happily fulfilled. At a time when the northern kingdom Israel had lost much of its territory to heathen conquests, Jonah prophesied that God would restore *the coast of Israel from the entering of Hamath unto the sea of the plain"* (2 Kings 14:25). This was accomplished during the reign over Israel of King Jeroboam II (believed to be from about 793 B.C. to 753 B.C.).

The prophecy, therefore, was uttered either early in the reign of Jeroboam II or in the latter years of his predecessor Jehoash, possibly around 790 B.C. The prophets Hosea and Amos were at least for a short time his contemporaries (note Hos. 1:1 and Amos 1:1). In addition, Jonah may well have known the prophet Elisha, whose ministry had extended into the times of Jehoash. It is even possible that Jonah could have been one of the *"sons of the prophets"* whom Elisha had trained (2 Kings 6:1–7). Thus, Jonah may well have been the first prophet chronologically of the 16 writers of the prophetical books of the Old Testament.

As an interesting aside, it may be that the father of Peter and Andrew, Christ's disciples, had been named after Jonah. Remember that Peter was known originally as Simon Bar-Jona (*"Simon, son of Jona"* Matt. 16:17; John 1:42). Jonah was definitely a much-revered prophet among the Jews at the time of Christ, as indicated by the two key references by Jesus to Jonah when rebuking the scribes and Pharisees (Matt. 12:40–41; see also Luke 11:29–32).

Since the kingdom of Assyria is prominent in Jonah's record, we need to review a little of its history and its situation at the time of Jonah. According to the biblical record, one of Shem's sons was Asshur, and the name Assyria undoubtedly comes from him (Gen. 10:22). It is reasonable to assume that he founded the city of Asshur, which (although it is never mentioned in the Bible) was the first capital of Assyria. Thus, Asshur was founder of Assyria, and the nation is occasionally called Asshur (e.g., Hos. 14:3). Asshur was also later deified as Assyria's chief god. One might speculate that Asshur originally tried to maintain the worship of his father's God there among his own family and followers, and that this was at least part of the incentive for him to leave Nimrod and Babel (Gen. 10:11).

Be that as it may, it wasn't long before Nimrod ventured from his own city, Babel, north into the region where Asshur had settled (that is, Assyria) and either founded or captured Nineveh, which would eventually become Assyria's capital and chief city. Like Asshur, it was near the banks of the Tigris River, about 100 miles north.

There seems to have been almost perpetual conflict between Assyria and Babylonia from the time of Nimrod on until Assyria was finally defeated decisively about 609 B.C., possibly originating in the fact that Nimrod was a Hamite, definitely in rebellion against God, while Asshur was a Semite, possibly seeking to defend faith in the God of his father Shem.

Speaking of Nimrod, the Genesis record says that *"the beginning of his kingdom was Babel, and Erech, and Accad, and Calneh, in the land of Shinar. Out of that land went forth Asshur, and builded Nineveh, and the city Rehoboth and Calah, And Resen between Nineveh and Calah: the same is a great city"* (Gen. 10:10–12).

These verses, as given in the King James translation, might indicate that Asshur himself built Nineveh, as well as Asshur. However, most Hebrew scholars argue that the correct translation of the first part of verse 12 should be: *"From that land* [that is, the land of Shinar and its capital Babel] *he* [that is, Nimrod] *went to Assyria and built Nineveh."*

If the latter translation is correct, then Nineveh was founded by Nimrod in the land of Assyria — which region had presumably been considered until then as part of Asshur's kingdom. Either way, it is clear that Nimrod took control of Assyria at this very early stage of its history, especially the city of Nineveh and its nearby cities. This must have been some time after the dispersion at Babel — enough time to develop substantial populations in other cities, especially those around Nineveh. One of these adjunct cities, Calah, is called a *"great city."* Its name, incidentally, later was changed to Nimrud — named after Nimrod, no doubt. In fact, much later, the nation of Assyria had come to be identified as *"the land of Nimrod"* (Mic. 5:6). By Micah's time, Nineveh was the capital of Assyria, and it was assumed by the Jews that Nimrod was its founder. Actually, the name Nineveh was probably derived from the god Ninus, which is believed to be another name of Nimrod, deified in Babylon after his death. Merodach (and Marduk) also were names of gods apparently based on the name of Nimrod.

It surely seems that Asshur and Nimrod (therefore, Assyria and Babylonia) were enemies right from the start. It seems possible, as noted above, that this enmity was occasioned in part by Asshur's desire to maintain belief in Jehovah, the God of his father, Shem. One wonders whether this might also have been true initially of Shem's other sons, Elam (ancestor of the Persians), Aram (ancestor of the Syrians), Lud (ancestor of the Lydians) and Arphaxad (ancestor of Terah and Abraham). For whatever significance it has, the Elamites and Aramaeans were also perennial enemies of the Babylonians.

In any case, whatever may have been their original status, all of these nations descended from Shem soon became polytheistic and morally depraved, like all the rest. Paul later reviewed the history of all the Gentile nations after Babel in these burning words: *". . . when they knew God, they glorified Him not as God, neither were thankful; but became vain in their imaginations, and their foolish heart was darkened. Professing themselves to be wise, they became fools, And changed the glory of the incorruptible God into an image made like to corruptible man, and to birds, and to fourfooted beasts, and creeping things. Wherefore God also gave them up to uncleanness through the lusts of their own hearts, to dishonour their own bodies between themselves: Who changed the truth of God into a lie, and worshipped and served the creature more than the Creator, who is blessed for ever. Amen"* (Rom. 1:21–25).

Between the time of Nimrod and Jonah (about 14 centuries), there had been many changes in the region, with almost perpetual fighting and movements among the nations. There is no purpose in reviewing all this history here. For those interested, there are numerous books available (e.g., *The Great Nations of Antiquity*).

With reference to Assyria in particular (as is true of the other ancient nations), most of our knowledge about her history has come from archaeological discoveries. Many inscribed tablets and monuments have been excavated at Nineveh, Calah, and other cities, so that Assyrian history is now reasonably well documented.

By the time of Jonah, Assyria had lost some of her former glory and influence and had not yet rebounded to her future period of still greater power, during which the ten tribes of the northern kingdom of Israel would be carried away into Assyrian exile (about 720 B.C.).

The actual preaching ministry of Jonah in Nineveh thus had to be sometime after the accession of King Jeroboam II over Israel (about 793 B.C.) and before the accession of Tiglath-Pelezer III over Assyria (about 745 B.C.), for the latter's reign marked the beginning of Assyria's period of greatest power and wickedness.

The weight of scholarly opinion is that Jonah's preaching in Nineveh occurred during the reign of Adad-Nirar III in Nineveh, which by then may have become Assyria's capital. His reign is said to have been about 810–783 B.C. However, scholarly opinion has been known sometimes to be wrong, and the Bible does not say. For our purposes, the precise date doesn't matter, so just say around 790 B.C.

There is no known extra-biblical record of the Ninevite revival, however, at this day or any other date (nor is there any denial anywhere of such a revival). In any case, this "argument from silence" surely cannot prevail against the divinely inspired record of the Bible, not to mention its later confirmation by the Lord Jesus Christ himself (see Matt. 12:41; Luke 11:32).

Therefore, as mentioned earlier, this brief commentary on the Book of Jonah is premised on the assumption that the account should be taken as historically true and, like all the Bible, should be taken literally unless the context indicates plainly that a symbolic or parabolic meaning is intended by the author.

Also, as noted above, it is significant that Jonah was a native of the tribal area assigned to Zebulon. This region was later a part of Galilee, proving that the Pharisees, thinking to rebuke Jesus, were wrong when they alleged that no prophet has arisen out of Galilee (John 7:52). In fact, there is a certain Jewish tradition (quite unverified, however) that Jonah was the son of the widow of Zarephath (1 Kings 17:8–24). Zarephath was in Phoenicia, but was adjacent to what later would be Galilee.

The Book of Jonah is a very short book, only four chapters and 48 verses in length. But it is a most fascinating book, and one with important lessons, not only for Jonah but for modern readers 2,600 years or more later.

TWO

RUNNING AWAY FROM GOD

Elijah and Elisha had departed from Israel — Elijah on a chariot of fire directly to heaven, Elisha by death. But Jonah was a proven prophet, and he was there. Israel had enjoyed a period of prosperity and expansion under King Jeroboam II, extending her boundaries north to the limit once attained under Solomon long before, and all this had been predicted by Jonah (2 Kings 14:25).

Surprisingly, however, God now had a unique mission for His prophet, one that Jonah would never have anticipated and which he did not relish at all.

JONAH 1:1-2

> *Now the word of the LORD came unto Jonah the son of Amittai, saying,*
> *Arise, go to Nineveh, that great city, and cry against it; for their wickedness is come up before me.*

When the word of the Lord came to Jonah this time, He did not tell Jonah to prophesy concerning Israel at all, as He had done before, but rather to arise and go to Nineveh, the chief city of the Assyrians, noted for the wickedness and cruelty of its inhabitants. There he was to preach against it and warn it of imminent judgment by God. The fact that Nineveh's wickedness had *"come up before me"* indicates that God was still concerned about all the nations, not just Israel. He was still *"the Judge of all the earth"* (Gen. 18:25), and was now about to judge Assyria.

Assyria was not then at the zenith of its power, but was obviously still a serious threat to neighboring countries. According to the prophet Hosea, who was a younger contemporary of Jonah in Israel, the nation had tried to enlist the aid of the Assyrians (Hos. 5:13; 7:11; 8:9; 12:1) against Syria. Instead of receiving help from Assyria, however, Israel *"shall be carried unto Assyria for a present to king Jareb"* (Hos. 10:6).

Whether Hosea's written prophecy had preceded Jonah's commission to Assyria is doubtful, but he had been prophesying bitterly against the sinfulness of Israel (in the midst of her great prosperity, no less) and it is not unlikely that Jonah had learned that an Assyrian invasion was a real threat. He did not want to go to Assyria — that's for sure!

Perhaps he realized it would be a very dangerous mission, for one thing. The cruel and licentious Assyrians could hardly be expected to receive an Israelite prophet warning them of their coming doom with a glad welcome. No telling what they would do to him.

Yet one does not get the impression that it was fear of personal harm that prompted Jonah's negative reaction to God's commission. He was not afraid to die, as evident from his later behavior on the ship of Tarshish. Rather it was his fear that the Ninevites might actually repent, and God would spare them (note Jon. 4:2).

Could it be, he may have asked himself, that the Ninevites might even replace Israel in God's favor? Israel had lately been falling into such depths of wickedness that God indeed might allow the Assyrians either to take them into captivity or even destroy them altogether. There must be some hidden reason why God would send an Israelite prophet to the Assyrians. He had never done this for any other Gentile nation, as far as the record goes.

There might even have been another question in Jonah's mind. How would his own countrymen react to such a mission? Jonah was well known and highly regarded. His activities could hardly be kept secret. Would his strange mission be regarded as somehow subversive or perhaps even treasonous?

Whatever the complex of reasons may have been, the end result was that Jonah, the divinely called prophet of God, made the dangerous decision to disobey God, and flee.

JONAH 1:3

> *But Jonah rose up to flee unto Tarshish from the presence of the LORD, and went down to Joppa; and he found a ship going to Tarshish: so he paid the fare thereof, and went down into it, to go with them unto Tarshish from the presence of the LORD.*

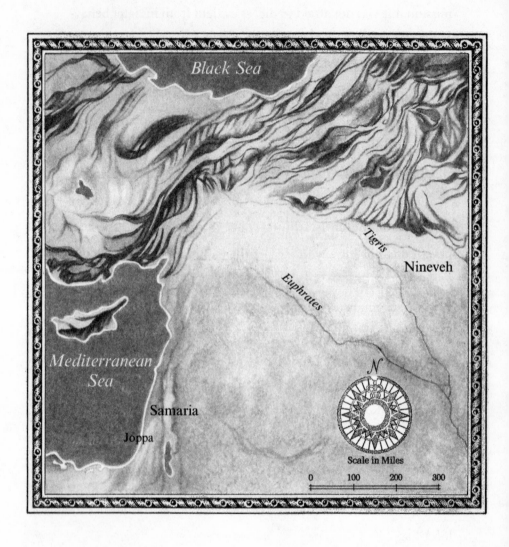

Instead of heading north and east toward that great city Nineveh, as God had told him, Jonah *"went down to Joppa,"* and then boarded a ship going far west *"unto Tarshish from the presence of the LORD"* (Jon. 1:3).

God had told Jonah to *"arise, go to Nineveh,"* so Jonah knew he could not simply continue where he was. He did *"arise,"* but not toward Nineveh; instead he *"rose up to flee unto Tarshish."*

Why Tarshish? For many centuries, scholars have been speculating about the location of Tarshish. It is generally agreed that it was a distant trading center established by the Phoenicians, probably at the outer extremity of their maritime journeyings. Jonah seems to have decided to get as far as possible away from Israel; perhaps God would forget about him there, and maybe decide it was not such a good idea to send an Israelite prophet to Nineveh after all.

Whatever Jonah's reasoning was, it was altogether wrong. Another great prophet, King David, had often faced dangerous decisions, and was tempted to flee. On one occasion, he wrote, *"Oh, that I had wings like a dove! for then would I fly away, and be at rest. Lo, then would I wander far off, and remain in the wilderness. Selah. I would hasten my escape from the windy storm and tempest"* (Ps. 55:6–8).

One wonders if Jonah may have thought about these words of David. After all, his very name (Jonah) meant "dove," and he may have thought a long-ranging ship journey would be to him the wings he needed. But David had also learned, as he wrote in another psalm, that *". . . whither shall I flee from thy presence? . . . If I take the wings of the morning, and dwell in the uttermost parts of the sea: Even there shall thy hand lead me, and thy right hand shall hold me"* (Ps. 139:7, 9–10). Jonah was surely about to learn this lesson in a most attention-grabbing manner!

Jonah could also have learned from the experience of still another great prophet, much closer to his own time. Elijah had (like Jonah) experienced a great prophetic victory in Israel, in the affair at Mount Carmel, where God defeated the prophets of Baal in spectacular fashion (1 Kings 18:22–46), calling down fire from God out of heaven.

But then, when Elijah heard that Queen Jezebel was after him to slay him, he *"arose, and went for his life"* (I Kings 19:3), fleeing all the way into the great wilderness south of Judah.

God found him even there, of course. Very soon afterwards, his prophetic mantle was transferred to Elisha, and Elijah was transferred to heaven. Jonah surely knew all this, but he fled anyway. Maybe Tarshish would be far enough away that the Lord would just leave him alone there. He surely knew the 139th psalm, however, and should have realized that he could not really escape God. Even *"if I make my bed in hell,"* David had said, and Jonah would soon find out for himself, *"behold, thou art there"* (Ps. 139:8).

Just where is Tarshish anyway? The small nation of Phoenicia, occupying a small strip of coastal land in what is now Lebanon, had become a great and prosperous nation because of the maritime commerce they developed. Also, it is often said that they invented alphabetic writing, which soon superseded pictographic, cuneiform, and hieroglyphic writing. They were descendants of Ham and had two great cities, Tyre and Sidon, which anchored their oceanic trade.

Despite their very small homeland, the Phoenicians were indisputably the leading mariners of the ancient world. There is much evidence that they sailed not only on the Persian Gulf and the Red Sea, but eventually all over the Mediterranean world and down the coast of Africa, even navigating around the tip of Africa and reaching the ports of India.

Consequently, they had trading centers all over the known world and were exceedingly prosperous. Tarshish was undoubtedly one of these. The greatest of these centers was at Carthage on the northern coast of North Africa. It eventually became a powerful nation itself, even threatening at one time to defeat the armies of the Roman Empire.

Although the name "Carthage" might conceivably be transmuted with time into "Tarshish," this is unlikely, and there is no direct evidence for it. It is intriguing to note, however, that Carthage was founded well before the time of Jonah, and yet is never mentioned in the Bible otherwise.

The name Tarshish (or Tharshish) is actually the name of one of the grandsons of Japheth. The Japhethites did largely settle in Europe, largely around the Mediterranean. It seems reasonable that the place named Tarshish was named after its founder, but that still doesn't say where it was. Some have suggested Italy.

There was a city in ancient Spain named Tartessos, and probably most authorities think this was Tarshish. Again there is no direct evidence. Many believe it was in Great Britain, and that the Phoenicians had developed a lucrative tin trade there.

There are, however, some intriguing passages of Scripture that suggest Tarshish was even farther away than Spain or Great Britain. In the time of King Solomon, when Hiram was king of Tyre (therefore, of Phoenicia), the remarkable cargo of one of these ships of Tarshish is mentioned. *"For the king had at sea a navy of*

Tharshish with the navy of Hiram: once in three years came the navy of Tharshish, bringing gold, and silver, ivory, and apes, and peacocks" (1 Kings 10:22).

Although this fleet belonged to Solomon, it was said to be a navy of Tarshish. The Phoenicians had developed such uniquely strong and competent ships for the long journey to Tarshish that they actually were called Tarshish ships, whether or not Tarshish was their home port. A three-year journey surely involved going farther than Spain or England. Further, the apes and ivory might have been obtained from somewhere in Africa, but the peacocks could only come from India.

As a matter of fact, there is indeed considerable evidence that the Phoenicians had acquired the ability to sail around the tip of Africa and all the way to India. They also plied the Red Sea and the Persian Gulf and could have reached India from one of these.

That is not all. Various writers have published archaeological findings in the Americas that bear strong similarities to Phoenician artifacts in other continents. Obviously this is controversial, but it may even be that the Phoenicians reached North and South America over a thousand years before Columbus or the Vikings. There is also that interesting reference to *"the merchants of Tarshish"* in connection with the invasion of Israel by Gog and Magog *"in the latter years"* (Ezek. 38:8,13). This is not the place to discuss such intriguing questions, however.

The main point here, of course, is that Jonah wanted to get as far away from Israel and God as he could, and that place was Tarshish, wherever it was. So he found one of these strong ships

The ships of Tarshish were strong and sturdy vessels of the Phoenicians, the leading mariners of the ancient world. Jonah was confident the ship he boarded would take him far from Nineveh and the uncomfortable presence of God.

of Tarshish down at Joppa and bought a ticket. It was, no doubt, a very expensive fare, but apparently his prophetic ministry, profitable as it had been to King Jeroboam, had made him reasonably affluent, so this was no problem.

Joppa was on the Mediterranean and was actually Jerusalem's main seaport, rather than Phoenicia's. It was about 35 miles northwest of Jerusalem, today known as Jaffa, the southern section of Tel Aviv. It had at one time been part of Philistia, but at this time was apparently under the control of Judah. At any rate, Jonah had to leave his own country of Israel to get there. Perhaps this was part of his planned escape route. His overriding purpose was *"to go with them unto Tarshish from the presence of the LORD,"* not stopping to think how futile that was.

Jonah was apparently tired from his trip (about 20 miles, on foot, from Samaria to Joppa, assuming he was living in or near Samaria, Israel's capital), so he went down into his quarters on the ship of Tarshish and settled in for the long journey, not yet realizing what an amazing journey it would turn out to be.

JONAH 1:4–5

> *But the LORD sent out a great wind into the sea, and there was a mighty tempest in the sea, so that the ship was like to be broken.*
>
> *Then the mariners were afraid, and cried every man unto his god, and cast forth the wares that were in the ship into the sea, to lighten it of them. But Jonah was gone down into the sides of the ship; and he lay, and was fast asleep.*

The account does not say where the ship was when the storm came up. They were no longer sailing along the coastline, which they would do as long as feasible, but were out in the open sea. Probably they were on the Mediterranean, although it is possible that they could have passed the Pillars of Hercules and were out in the Atlantic. It had apparently been a peaceful trip to this point, for Jonah was down in his quarters fast asleep. Perhaps God was giving Jonah a little more time to think over what he was doing and then decide to turn back.

In any case, a sudden storm arose, and it was a great storm, more severe than these experienced sailors had ever encountered. Any crew manning a ship of Tarshish was undoubtedly one of great ability and long experience. They had successively weathered many storms in the past, but this one was different! It had been generated directly by God himself. Try as they could, they could not maintain control of the ship under such blows.

One almost inevitably thinks of another sudden storm, many centuries later, on the little sea of Galilee, in Jonah's home country. On that occasion, Jesus — not Jonah — was asleep in the boat while the disciples, several of them seasoned fishermen, tried to keep it afloat. When they awakened Jesus and asked Him to do something, He *"rebuked the wind, and said unto the sea, Peace, be still. And the wind ceased, and there was a great calm"* (Mark 4:39). *"What manner of man is this,"* the disciples whispered among themselves, *"that even the wind and the sea obey Him?"* (Mark 4:41).

He was, in fact, the very one who had created the sea and the wind, and He was the one who had generated Jonah's tempest as well. *"All things were made by Him"* (John 1:3), and one cannot escape the will of God by fleeing toward Tarshish.

> *For He commandeth, and raiseth the stormy wind, which lifteth up the waves thereof.*
>
> *They mount up to the heaven, they go down again to the depths: their soul is melted because of trouble.*
>
> *They reel to and fro, and stagger like a drunken man, and are at their wit's end.*
>
> *Then they cry unto the LORD in their trouble, and He bringeth them out of their distresses,*
>
> *He maketh the storm a calm, so that the waves thereof are still* (Ps. 107:25–29).

The mariners on Jonah's ship could not pray to *"the LORD"* — that is, to Jehovah, the God who controlled the sea — for they did not know Him, but they were each crying out to his own god. They were not all Phoenicians, but expert seamen from various nations, but their gods could not help.

They even tossed overboard all their valuable cargo of goods, thinking this would help. That decision was a mirror of their desperate concern, for the valuable cargo was the reason for their journey in the first place.

Then they discovered that their one passenger was fast asleep! How he could sleep under such conditions is a mystery, but at any rate, they forthwith roused him and told him that he should pray to *his* god. Quite possibly, they realized that Jonah worshiped the God of Israel, whom the Israelites claimed to be the Creator of heaven and earth. If there was any possibility that the Israelites were right about this, then Jonah, by all means, was the one who should be praying. At any rate, *their* gods were not helping.

Their ship was as sturdy as any ship made in those days, having been designed to sail all the way to Tarshish. All their "wares" had been thrown into the sea, so the forces on the ship, apart from the hydrodynamic impact of the waves, were minimal, yet the ship was being hammered and tossed so severely that they feared it would soon break into pieces and they would all be drowned.

JONAH 1:6–7

> *So the shipmaster came to him, and said unto him, What meanest thou, O sleeper? arise, call upon thy God, if so be that God will think upon us, that we perish not.*
>
> *And they said every one to his fellow, Come, and let us cast lots, that we may know for whose cause this evil is upon us. So they cast lots, and the lot fell upon Jonah.*

The captain of the ship probably knew more about Jonah than any of the others, and he felt it was urgent for Jonah to be up and praying to God. They had never before encountered so severe a storm as this one, and this strange passenger was the only new variable. They may well have sensed that the storm had something to do with Jonah being on board. In any event, he should be praying, not sleeping!

Jonah, by this time, must also have begun to realize the same thing, and as he prayed, God must have told him somehow that

But the LORD sent out a great wind into the sea, and there was a mighty tempest in the sea, so that the ship was like to be broken" (Jon. 1:4). Jonah, whose name means "dove," had thought he would *"fly away, and be at rest"* (Ps. 55:6), but one should never trifle with the known will of God.

the storm would only cease when he turned around and headed for Nineveh.

However, he realized that such a request to the shipmaster would certainly be refused. For the captain to return to Joppa with his cargo all gone and nothing to show for it would not only be very costly to his employers but would surely result in the rude discharge of the captain and his whole crew — possibly even imprisonment or worse. The only thing *they* could do — that is, if the ship survived at all — was to go on to Tarshish in hopes that their trading partners there would extend them enough credit to enable them to return with a reasonable cargo of tin or such other products as would be suitable. So, as far as we know, Jonah did not even propose that they just return to Joppa.

In the meantime, the crew, suspecting that the problem was Jonah, yet wanting to be sure, decided to cast lots. And, sure enough, the lot fell on Jonah. He was the cause.

And Jonah admitted it. He told them all about his divine call to preach in Nineveh and then his decision not to obey.

JONAH 1:8-10

> *Then said they unto him, Tell us, we pray thee, for whose cause this evil is upon us; What is thine occupation? and whence comest thou? what is thy country? and of what people art thou?*
>
> *And he said unto them, I am an Hebrew; and I fear the LORD, the God of heaven, which hath made the sea and the dry land.*

Then were the men exceedingly afraid, and said unto him, Why hast thou done this? For the men knew that he fled from the presence of the LORD, because he had told them.

Regardless of what we think of Jonah's decision to flee from God's mission for him, we must acknowledge his courageous testimony before these heathen sailors. It is interesting that he called himself, *"an Hebrew,"* rather than an Israelite or a Zebulonite. That was a much broader term, of course, being derived from the name Eber, the great, great, great, great grandfather of Abraham. Although there could be a number of other tribes descended from Eber, the name Hebrew has somehow come to be so identified with the descendants of Jacob (or Israel) that no one else seems ever to have laid claim to it.

Jonah was clearly a creationist. Most of the pantheistic religions of the ancients could properly be called evolutionary religions, since they offered no explanation for the origin of the space-time-matter universe, although offering various bizarre explanations of how "gods," animals and people may have emerged from the primeval chaos.

Jonah, however, frankly stressed that he worshiped the *"god of heaven,"* who had *"made the sea and the dry land"* and who certainly could control the sea and the winds stirring it up, if He so chose. He acknowledged that the Lord was angry with him and had sent the terrible storm on his account, just as their lot-casting had shown.

To us today, the casting of lots seems an odd — even super-stitious — way of determining answers to questions. We have, especially in the New Testament, wonderful guidelines for deter-mining God's will in a given matter, so why resort to some pseudo-gambling device (casting lots, drawing straws, throwing dice, toss-ing a coin, etc.).

Nevertheless, the Old Testament in particular has many in-stances where God led in a decision by the casting of lots (e.g., the case of Achan, recorded in Josh. 7:10–18). Even in the New Tes-tament (though actually before any of it had been written), the casting of lots was used to determine whether Matthias or Barsabas should take the place of Judas among the twelve apostles (Acts 1:24–26). They did pray first, however, asking the Lord to indi-cate His will this way.

There is even a relevant verse on this subject in the Book of Proverbs *"The lot is cast into the lap; but the whole disposing thereof is of the LORD"* (Prov. 16:33).

As to just what these "lots" which were being cast may have been, no one seems to know for certain. Small colored stones, analogous to our modern dice cubes, have often been suggested. Possibly different devices were used, depending on the situation. Anything that could be "thrown" randomly and without bias would probably do.

A mere random choice would hardly be appropriate in mak-ing an important spiritual decision today, unless there seemed no other way of arriving at the decision. At the very least, such a means of deciding should be preceded by earnest prayer — as in the case of Matthias. The Lord is certainly as free to lead His people in this way, if He so wills, but normally there are more spiritually meaningful ways of determining God's will, for those who truly want to know it.

In any event, the casting of lots in Jonah's case did work, as God so overruled, and Jonah admitted that he indeed was their problem. The immediate question now was how to solve that problem. But Jonah already had a solution.

THREE

THE WHALE-WAY EXPRESS

By this time, Jonah surely was sorry that he had tried to run away from God. Not only was he about to die, but so were all the mariners he had been counting on to take him to Tarshish. If all this had not generated true repentance, it is hard to imagine what would. He was now willing to go to Nineveh, but how could he get there? The ship of Tarshish could hardly be asked to return to Joppa, or go to some port nearer to Nineveh, even if the ship-master would or could consider such a demand. With his valuable cargo jettisoned, that poor captain, now afraid that his entire ship was about to be lost, must have been beside himself and was devoting all his attention and efforts simply to get the ship to a safe landing somewhere.

As Jonah prayed, asking forgiveness and expressing his willingness now to preach in Nineveh, one wonders whether the Lord somehow may have told him just to leave the ship and trust God to get him to Assyria. At any rate, that's what happened!

Then said they unto him, What shall we do unto thee,
that the sea may be calm unto us? for the sea wrought, and
was tempestuous,

And he said unto them, Take me up, and cast me forth
into the sea; so shall the sea be calm unto you: for I know that
for my sake this great tempest is upon you.

How did Jonah *know* that the storm would cease once he was off the ship? Whether the ship at this time was on the Mediterranean or the Atlantic, great tempests occur rather frequently on both seas, and many ships, both ancient and recent, now lie at the bottom of their deep waters. Jonah might have suspected that God had sent the storm on account of his presence, but he seemed quite certain that God would say: *"Peace, be still,"* to the raging waters once Jonah was in them. How did he know?

And how could he so calmly tell the sailors to send him to his death? One would think that he would resist with all his might any decision on their part to dispose of him thus.

There is an implication that Jonah had heard from God! Jonah had heard the voice of God telling him to arise and go to Nineveh while he was back in Israel, so it would not be unlikely that God would speak to him once again, and this would be the time to do it. Jonah was now willing to go to Nineveh, but he could never get there this way, so God somehow told him what to do, and — incidentally — how to save the lives of all the mariners.

When Elijah was fleeing Jezebel, God finally spoke to him in a *"still, small voice"* (1 Kings 19:12). God's message of rebuke to Elijah had been: *"What doest thou here, Elijah?"* (1 Kings 19:13). The same question would have been appropriate for Jonah, but it could hardly be a still, small voice this time, with all the thunderous sounds of the storm about him. Possibly God spoke in the thunder, as He did many years later when Saul was going to Damascus to try to stamp out the new Christian sect that had arisen after Christ's death and resurrection. The people that were with Saul (later to be re-named Paul) could hear a voice but not the message (Acts 9:7). When God on one occasion spoke to His Son from heaven, those who were standing by thought it was thunder (John 12:28–29).

The fact is that God has spoken in different ways on different occasions. God *"at sundry times and in divers manners spake in time past"* (Heb. 1:1). How — or whether — He spoke to Jonah at this time, Jonah has not said, but somehow Jonah learned what he must do, and this time he followed orders!

JONAH 1:13–15

> *Nevertheless the men rowed hard to bring it to the land;*
> *but they could not: for the sea wrought, and was tempestuous*
> *against them.*
>
> *Wherefore they cried unto the LORD, and said, We beseech thee, O LORD, we beseech thee, let us not perish for this*
> *man's life, and lay not upon us innocent blood: for thou, O*
> *LORD, hast done as it pleased thee.*

So they took up Jonah, and cast him forth into the sea:
and the sea ceased from her raging.

Jonah's willingness to die for their sakes evidently made quite an impression on these hardened mariners, and they worked all the harder to get the boat toward land without having to resort to such extreme measure. All they could do was to man the oars vigorously; their sails were useless in such violent and variable winds, and they had long since been furled. But their most strenuous rowing efforts were not doing any good either, and it soon became clear that nothing less than a divine miracle could save them.

But all their own gods to whom they had been praying earnestly also seemed helpless. Jonah had told them about his mission from "*the LORD,*" and had told them that *his* God ("*the LORD*" — that is Jehovah or Yahweh) not only had sent the storm in the first place, but also that He was "*the LORD, the God of heaven, which hath made the sea and the dry land* " (Jon. 1:9). It was obvious that the sea, which He had made, was now acting "*against them,*" and so they had better do what Jonah said.

At this point, Jonah, who had been a backslidden prophet running away from God, now becomes a true type of Christ. "*As Jonas . . . so shall the Son of man*" (Matt. 12:40), said the Lord Jesus Christ, thereby indicating that we may legitimately see here in Jonah (or Jonas) a real type of the eventual coming of Christ and His work to save sinners. He must die, so they could live. This was what the repentant prophet told the sailors, and in desperation they believed him. They all forgot their own futile gods and called on Jehovah. *"We beseech thee, O LORD,"* they cried, *"let us not perish for this man's life."*

The prophet Joel had promised that *"whosoever shall call on the name of the LORD shall be delivered "*(Joel 2:32), and this promise was later repeated and applied to eternal salvation through Christ by Peter (Acts 2:21) and by Paul (Rom. 10:13). The pagan mariners, therefore, not only were saved from death in the raging waters but (it is reasonable to believe) from eternal damnation through trusting in the true Creator God.

Pagan though their backgrounds may have been, they seem to have retained enough of the primeval revelation to know that murder was punishable by death. Deliberately sending Jonah to die in the sea would seem like killing an innocent man — in fact, a man who had paid handsomely for the journey and was trusting them to take him to his destination. Therefore, they prayed to Jehovah: *". . . lay not upon us innocent blood."*

Even though Jonah had offered to die, they were reluctant to cast him into the sea, but so it must be. The Lord evidently had instructed Jonah not simply to jump into the sea on his own but rather to instruct the sailors to carry out the lethal deed. Just so, the Lord Jesus could not just commit suicide, but must be *"delivered into the hands of men, and they shall kill him . . ."*(Mark 9:31).

So Jonah was not to kill himself, but to be killed. Thus, regardless of the circumstances, the mariners were guilty of murder when they threw him overboard. Similarly, Pilate could proclaim, *"I am innocent of the blood of this just person,"* but he was guilty nonetheless, for *"when he had scourged Jesus, he delivered him to be crucified "*(Matt. 27:24, 26).

J onah knew the deadly storm had been sent because

of him. Not wanting to cause the death of the sailors also, he

urged them to cast him into the waves, so finally *"They took Jonah,*

and cast him forth into the sea, and the sea ceased from her raging"

(Jon. 1:15).

In the case of Jonah, however, the mariners had placed their faith in the true God and were, in effect, consciously appropriating the substitutionary death of Jonah as payment for their own deliverance. Similarly, we today in a very real sense are guilty personally of putting Christ to death since He *"was delivered for our offences"* (Rom. 4:25) and *"died for our sins"* (1 Cor. 15:3).

Yet, in an amazing transaction, when we truly believe that He somehow was able to *"overcome evil with good "*(Rom. 12:21), as God *"made Him to be sin for us"* (though He himself *"knew no sin"*), we are *"made the righteousness of God in him"* (2 Cor. 5:21). Similarly, in type, the Phoenician mariners, though guilty of murder when they sent Jonah to a drowning death, nevertheless were saved by God's grace as they trusted and obeyed His word.

JONAH 1:16

> *Then the men feared the LORD exceedingly, and offered a sacrifice unto the LORD, and made vows.*

The genuineness of the new-found faith of these ancient mariners is demonstrated by their behavior after the sea stopped its raging. Unlike many new "converts" to Christianity today, whose post-conversion life is hardly any different from before, their actions showed that they not only believed on Jehovah as the true God of creation but also they were beginning, at least, to comprehend the truth of redemption. Their own lives had been redeemed from destruction, but it had cost the life of Jonah (the "dove").

They proceeded to offer a sacrifice to Jehovah, the God of Jonah. We are not told what they offered. It seems unlikely that they had on board any sheep or goats to offer, but could it have been a gentle dove, perhaps in thankfulness to Jonah's memory? Doves were widely used for both food and sacrifice (especially by the poor) in the ancient world, both in Israel and other countries.

Maybe they were also reminded, as mariners, of the oft-told tale of the great Flood, and how Noah had sent forth a dove from the ark to determine whether the ground was dry enough for them to venture forth into that new world. In contrast, Jonah the "dove" had been sent forth, not to explore the ocean, but to bring peace to it.

In any case, a dove would have provided an ideal sacrifice and acknowledgment of the true God of heaven there after the storm ceased its raging. These new converts feared the Lord *exceedingly*, it says, thus indicating a passionate, life-changing commitment to Jehovah. One wonders what vows they made. Did they become proselytes to Israel? More likely, they simply resolved to make Jehovah God *their* God from then on, serving Him and obeying His Word.

Perhaps these Phoenician mariners (Phoenician in terms of their ship, that is, but actually from various nations in terms of their respective genealogies) could be considered as a sort of "firstfruits" of the great harvest that would accrue to Jonah once he reached Nineveh. The god of the Phoenicians had been Baal, but Elijah's God, Jehovah, had thoroughly defeated and discredited Baal at the contest on Mount Carmel not too many years before this (see 1 Kings 18). Now the impotence of Baal and the other idol gods, in relation to that same mighty God of heaven — now known by the mariners to be Jonah's God as well as Elijah's

— made such an indelible impression on them that they *"feared the* LORD *exceedingly"* and could never be the same again.

We don't know whether or not they continued their journey to Tarshish, but wherever they went, we can be sure they told the amazing story of Jonah and the storm. They themselves, however, did not yet know the even more fantastic end of the story!

JONAH 1:17

Now the LORD *had prepared a great fish to swallow up Jonah. And Jonah was in the belly of the fish three days and three nights.*

At this point in the story, obviously presented by the writer as a simple factual record of what happened, we encounter the skeptics. The entire account is impossible, they say, and so must be treated as a legend or as an allegory or as anything but sober history.

No whale has a gullet large enough to swallow a man whole, they argue, and even if this was some unknown sea monster that could actually swallow a man, he could not possibly survive for three days and three nights in its belly, then emerge and proceed on to conduct a powerful preaching mission in the great metropolis of Nineveh, even turning the whole wicked city into a God-fearing community. Absurd!

So quit trying to make out that all this really happened, they say, and get on to the spiritual message the writer was trying to convey in his allegorical legend, whatever it could be. Or else just ignore it altogether. The Book of Jonah is a very small book and possibly should not even have been included among the prophetical books of the Old Testament — so say the skeptics and liberal theologians.

The problem is that it *has* been included in the canon of Scripture, by Jewish and Christian scholars alike, all through the centuries. It *cannot* be ignored.

An even greater problem with the non-historical view of Jonah is that the Lord Jesus Christ endorsed it as true history, and even as a typological precursor to His own future experience. *"For as Jonas was three days and three nights in the whale's belly; so shall the Son of man be three days and three nights in the heart of the earth"* (Matt. 12:40). That was the assertion of Christ.

Now, Jesus Christ had claimed to be equal with God the Father, as His only begotten Son, on many occasions and in many ways. While the skeptic is ready to charge Him with falsehood or insanity or something comparable, He could not have claimed Jonah's record to be true unless it really happened. The Lord Jesus Christ would surely *know* whether the story of Jonah was real history or not and He would surely speak the truth about what He knew, and *He* says it really happened! That should be enough for the Christian.

Therefore, we should settle in our minds that Jonah really was swallowed by a whale and survived, coming forth later alive and well. Actually, Jonah's account merely calls this animal a "great fish" [Hebrew *gadol dag*], where the word *dag* is the ordinary Hebrew word for "fish." This fish was not an ordinary fish, however, but a *great* fish. The adjective "great" is used no less than seven times in the small book of Jonah ("great wind," "great tempest," "great fish," and "great city," the latter occurring four times, always referring to Nineveh). It is obvious that this was a *great* fish.

The fact that modern biologists do not regard the whale as a fish, but as a marine mammal, is not relevant. The biblical classification system is based on different criteria than the modern Linnaean system. Marine vertebrates are "fish" in the Bible, whether or not they are warm blooded and suckle their young.

Jonah's whale, as far as Jonah's record itself is concerned, could have been any kind of sea creature prepared by God for this special purpose, *"The LORD had prepared a great fish,"* it says.

The reference in Matthew 12:40 to the words of Christ, however, does appear to be more definitive. There the word is the Greek *ketos*, used only this one time in the New Testament, however. Many expositors say it could be used for any great monster of the sea.

Assuming it to have been a whale, it is still not correct to say that no whale has a gullet large enough to admit a man. There are many species of whales (some of the larger ones now being extinct, preserved only in fossil form), and some are very large. One notable example is the sperm whale, which does exist in both Atlantic and Mediterranean waters. This animal has an enormous head, with a gullet certainly large enough to swallow a man. In fact, it is known to swallow large sharks and porpoises. There have even been a number of reports in the lore of the whaling industry of men swallowed by such whales, later being found still alive in their stomachs. These tales, however, have commonly been debunked on closer investigation, and are irrelevant anyhow.

As to whether a man could survive three days in such a situation, it does not seem impossible. The large whales ingest tremendous quantities of air, and can retain it for long periods. Again, however, there is no reason to try to explain Jonah's experience on a naturalistic basis, since the Bible clearly describes the whole event as a miracle. This particular "fish" — whether whale or whale-shark or ichthyosaur or some other sea-monster — was a special fish *prepared* by God for a very special mission. The Hebrew word for "prepared" [*manah*] is only translated "prepared" in Jonah. It seems to imply careful design and weighing.

This particular great fish had been commissioned by its Creator to provide transportation for Jonah back toward Nineveh! On another occasion, centuries later, another fish was commissioned to swallow a coin and retain it long enough to provide money for the governmental taxes required from Jesus and His followers (Matt. 17:24–27). If *"even the wind and the sea obey Him"* (Mark 4:41), is it surprising that the fish of the sea also do so?

Jonah needed urgently to head back toward Nineveh, and there was no ship or bus or any other vehicle to take him there. Therefore, the God of heaven and earth, in whose service he was, prepared a very special vehicle to take him on as a very special passenger.

This did not happen immediately. Jonah undoubtedly was fully clothed and probably had with him whatever possessions he owned and was planning to take to Tarshish. Thus, when the mariners cast him overboard, he certainly did not remain near the sea's surface, but plummeted rapidly to the bottom, retaining consciousness for a few moments, but probably eventually drowning.

When the whale, directed by God, finally reached him, it quickly engulfed his body whole, seating it in some inner pocket where it could resist both the digestive processes acting on the whale's food and also the beginning of corruptive activity in Jonah's own body.

In the meantime, as we shall see in the next chapter, the soul/spirit of Jonah had descended into sheol, or hades, while his dead body, resting in the whale's belly, was being transported back toward Nineveh.

The account has not told us where the ship was when Jonah was thrown overboard. Therefore, we don't know how far it was from Nineveh. For that matter, the whale could have brought Jonah straight back to Joppa, rather than to a more northerly point on the eastern shore.

In any event, the sperm whale (or whatever the "great fish" might have been) is able to descend to great depths and to swim at great speeds. Apparently the journey was one which would take three days and three nights when traveling by whale express!

Who measured that time, by the way? Jonah could hardly have kept track of it himself. Even if he had been alive and conscious, it was all night to him where he was.

Somehow Jonah learned later how long his body had lain in the whale's belly, and it does seem that no one could have known this except God himself. Therefore, God must have told him when He spoke to Jonah again. Presumably there was a reason why God wanted this little item of information recorded in His Word. There had been a mighty miracle — or series of miracles — regardless of the length of time involved.

It is hard to come to any conclusion on this little question without thinking of Jonah as a type of Christ. We have referred already more than once to Matthew 12:40. Jonah could not know (apart from revelation) that over half a millennium later, his God would become a man and then die and rise again — much as Jonah had. And the time involved would be the same in both cases. Whatever exact number of hours and minutes is meant by *"three days and three nights,"* the body of the Lord Jesus Christ would lie in a borrowed tomb the same length of time Jonah's body had rested in a prepared fish. Jonah would become a living testimony to his own generation that Jehovah was indeed the Creator and Restorer of life, just as the Lord Jesus Christ would eventually to *every* generation, for *His* resurrection is the most surely established fact of all history.

FOUR

THREE DAYS
AND THREE NIGHTS

The account says plainly that *"Jonah was in the belly of the fish three days and three nights"* (Jon. 1:17). Since there is no way that either he or the mariners could have measured the time, it is assumed that God gave Jonah that information later, probably because it somehow would provide some special insight into the underlying purpose of Jonah's experience and his book.

As noted earlier, it is possible that Jonah was the first book written of the 17 books of the prophets (Isaiah through Malachi). Jonah wrote the prophecy recorded in 2 Kings 14:25 during the days of King Joash of Israel, while Israel was struggling against the invading Syrians. This was soon after the ministries of Elijah and Elisha, the great prophets who had tried hard to call Israel back to God, largely without success despite the mighty miracles which God performed by their hands. Neither Elijah nor Elisha were among the writing prophets, of course. And, although Jonah's book was written during the reign of the next king, Jeroboam II, it strangely contains no prophetic material except one verse of prophetic warning to Nineveh (Jon. 3:4).

But there is this one very special verse about three days and three nights, apparently revealed by God directly, then eventually quoted by Christ, and cited as a miraculous prophetic sign of his own coming death, burial, and resurrection. This alone would warrant the inclusion of the Book of Jonah among the books of the prophets — indeed the very first of those books chronologically. Of course, the prophecy of 2 Kings 14:25, fulfilled during the reign of Jeroboam II over Israel, had already marked Jonah as a true prophet.

There are some other unique features of the Book of Jonah which warrant mention. It is the only one of the 17 books of the prophets which makes no mention whatever of either Israel or Judah, yet the Jewish scholars have always included it in their canon of Scripture, as one of the holy books of Israel and Judah.

It is focused altogether on their bitter enemy, the nation of Assyria and its great city Nineveh. And strangely, although predicting Nineveh's destruction, it seems aimed primarily at the goal of Assyria's conversion. In fact, Jonah was the only one of the 16 writing prophets (one prophet wrote both Jeremiah and Lamentations) who was directed by God to go and preach to a pagan nation. It is a remarkable book in many ways.

But back to the matter of the three days and three nights. If this is taken literally to mean three 24-hour periods, then Jonah's body would have been in the belly of the whale for 72 long hours. In turn, that would mean that Christ's body had lain in Joseph's tomb for 72 hours. Christ's prophecy in Matthew 12:40 seemed to indicate clearly and emphatically that the two times were to be identical. *"As Jonas was three days and three nights in the whale's belly; so shall the Son of man be three days and three nights in the heart of the earth"* (Matt. 12:40).

However, the testimony of long tradition and practice is that, although three days were involved, the actual time began with Jesus' burial late on a Friday evening and resurrection early on Sunday morning — a total of perhaps 30 hours. Churches down through the centuries have recognized His crucifixion and burial on "Good Friday" and His resurrection on Easter Sunday. Is this all wrong?

We do not want to depend too much on tradition, of course, but traditions start sometime somewhere, and no one seems able to pinpoint when this one started, unless it *was* the belief of the early Jewish churches that began soon after the great events themselves, while many people were still alive and knew the facts.

Furthermore, the four gospel records of the death, burial, and resurrection of Christ give no hint that the period of interment was nearly as long as three whole days and three whole nights. Each of the four writers — Matthew, Mark, Luke, and John — indicate that Jesus' body was buried late on the day of the preparation for the sabbath. For example, Mark's account tells us that He was buried *"when the even was come, because it was the preparation, that is, the day before the sabbath"* (Mark 15:42). There was some degree of haste necessary, because no work could be done (certainly no burials) on the sabbath. The word "sabbath," incidentally, simply means "rest."

The body of Jesus then also rested in the grave throughout the entire sabbath night and day. Most scholars believe that the Jewish day *began* in the evening, patterned after the creation account in Genesis, where it says that *"the evening and the morning were the first day"* (Gen. 1:5).

Once again, all four writers — Matthew, Mark, Luke, and John — agree that the resurrection took place sometime earlier than when Christ's women followers intending to anoint His body *"very early in the morning the first day of the week, they came unto the sepulchre at the rising of the sun"* (Mark 16:2), and He was already gone. Actually, Mary of Magdala had come even earlier *"when it was yet dark"* and later actually met the risen Lord at the graveside (John 20:1, 14).

There is no hint in any of the four Gospel accounts of Christ's death and resurrection that any additional time was involved. According to them, He was crucified on the day before the sabbath, rested in the tomb throughout the sabbath day of rest, then rose from the dead very early the day after the sabbath — that is, the first day of the week. There is no hint of any additional time involved. He died on Friday and rose on Sunday, at least as best as we can determine through the four narrative accounts in the Gospels.

And yet, Jesus did say *"three days and three nights in the heart of the earth."* Is this a contradiction? A considerable number of scholars, insisting that the statement of Christ must be taken literally, have sought to resolve the problem by assuming Christ died *before* Friday — some say Thursday; many say Wednesday. The key, they say, is to recognize that there was more than one sabbath involved on that week of the Passover. That is, the sabbath following the day of Christ's crucifixion was not the same as the sabbath day just prior to His resurrection.

The events all were taking place at the Passover season, and it is true that two special sabbaths were associated with the Passover — one at the feast of the Passover itself (on the 14th day of the first month), one at the Feast of Unleavened Bread, on the day following. On both of these feast days, no servile work (that is no occupational work) was to be done. On the weekly sabbath, however, no work of any kind was to be done. It has been assumed by some that all three sabbaths occurred successively (on Thursday, Friday, and Saturday) on that week of Christ's crucifixion. Thus, assuming that Christ died on Wednesday, there would be three days and three nights before He rose from the dead early Sunday morning.

This might be a solution. However, it requires a rather arbitrary arrangement of the days of the week to correlate with the required monthly dates for the two feasts, of Passover and unleavened bread. This sequence could occur occasionally but there is no certainty that it occurred in the year Christ died. In fact, the year itself is uncertain, as is the year of His birth.

The use of the term *"high day"* in John 19:31 has been taken by some to mean the special sabbath day at the time of Passover, but the fact is that there was no "higher day" in the Jewish system than the weekly sabbath, when no work of any kind was supposed to be done. In context, that weekly holy sabbath certainly seems the most likely "high day" to be honored.

This type of argument has been developed with cogency by some very competent Bible teachers, however, and no doubt has significant merit.

However, it does not really deal compellingly with the strong evidence for the Friday crucifixion long held by most Christians through the ages. Furthermore, it does not deal adequately with the oft-repeated promise that Christ would be raised on the third day.

In fact, that assertion is made so many times in the New Testament (in contrast to the one-time-only mention of three days and three nights) that there would seem to be a special and intentional emphasis on the fact that Christ would rise *on* the third day, not *after* the three days and three nights. Because of their significance, it seems worthwhile to list *all* these references, in numerical order as found in the New Testament.

The first occurs immediately after Peter's great confession that Jesus was *"the Christ, the Son of the living God "*(Matt. 16:16).

(1)   *From that time forth began Jesus to shew unto his disciples, how that he must go unto Jerusalem, and suffer many things of the elders and chief priests and scribes, and be killed, and be raised again the third day* (Matt. 16:21).

This surely seems to indicate that he would be raised the third day after being killed, presumably on the first day. Later, while still in Galilee, Jesus said:

(2)   *The Son of man shall be betrayed into the hands of men: And they shall kill him, and the third day he shall be raised again* (Matt. 17:22–23).

Later, as they began to head toward Jerusalem for this confrontation, He told them again:

> (3) *Behold, we go up to Jerusalem; and the Son of man shall be betrayed unto the chief priests and unto the scribes, and they shall condemn him to death, And shall deliver him to the Gentiles to mock, and to scourge, and to crucify him: and the third day he shall rise again* (Matt. 20:18–19).

Mark, in his gospel, apparently repeats the same promise Matthew had recorded (although Mark may possibly have been written chronologically before Matthew). This was during the considerable time that they were in Galilee, however, so it could actually have been a separate occasion.

> (4) *For he taught his disciples, and said unto them, The Son of man is delivered into the hands of men, and they shall kill him; and after that he is killed, he shall rise the third day* (Mark 9:31).

Mark also reported the conversation on the way to Jerusalem.

> (5) *Behold, we go up to Jerusalem; and the Son of man shall be delivered unto the chief priests, and unto the scribes; and they shall condemn him to death, and shall deliver him to the Gentiles: And they shall mock him, and shall scourge him, and shall spit upon him, and*

shall kill him: and the third day he shall rise again (Mark 10:33–34).

Luke, in his gospel, also records this prophecy on two occasions.

(6) *The Son of man must suffer many things, and be rejected of the elders and chief priests and scribes, and be slain, and be raised the third day* (Luke 9:22).

(7) *For he shall be delivered unto the Gentiles, and shall be mocked, and spitefully entreated, and spitted on: And they shall scourge him, and put him to death: and the third day he shall rise again* (Luke 18:32–33).

There are no specific references in John's gospel to a third-day resurrection, but probably the first of all Christ's predictions of His own resurrection is found there in essentially equivalent words.

(8) *Jesus answered and said unto them, Destroy this temple, and in three days* [note — not *after* three days] *I will raise it up. . . . But He spake of the temple of His body* (John 2:19–21).

Thus there were at least seven references in the four Gospels to Christ being raised on the third day, representing at least five different occasions. Peter and Paul also refer to it once each, as already fulfilled. In his important message to the Roman centurion and his family, the Apostle Peter said, speaking of Christ:

> (9)   *And we are witnesses of all things which he did both in the land of the Jews, and in Jerusalem; whom they slew and hanged on a tree: Him God raised up the third day, and shewed him openly* (Acts 10:39–40).

Similarly, the Apostle Paul, in writing to the church at Corinth, referred to this great event as the climactic part of the saving gospel of Christ.

> (10)   *For I delivered unto you first of all that which I also received, how that Christ died for our sins according to the scriptures; And that he was buried, and that he rose again the third day according to the scriptures* (1 Cor. 15:3–4).

Thus there are no less than nine(!) references in the New Testament to Christ being raised from the dead on *"the third day."* This seems clearly to contrast with the one single statement in Matthew 12:40 that the Lord Jesus Christ would *"be three days and three nights in the heart of the earth."*

There is one reference indicating that His resurrection would be *"after three days"* (Mark 8:31), and this was the way His enemies later reported His claim (e.g., Matt. 27:63). However, the Jewish leaders, who reported this claim to Pilate, only asked *"the sepulchre be made sure until the third day"* (Matt. 27:64), indicating that they understood that *"after three days"* really had the same meaning to any listeners as *"the third day"* (literally), so they had obviously understood that the prophecy really only applied *through* the third day, not *after* the third day.

Thus, it becomes obvious that at least one of the two forms of the prediction was intended to be taken loosely rather than literally. Christ could not spend a literal 72 hours in the tomb (that is, three days and three nights) and also be raised on the third day. He could not be raised *on* the third day and also *after* three days.

Either *"three days and three nights"* was just an idiomatic way of saying "parts of three contiguous days" (as most evangelical scholars would argue), or else *"raised the third day"* somehow could mean "raised after three full days and nights." Both expressions could not be *literally* true, so one must choose.

The weight of evidence (universal tradition, the straightforward records in the four Gospels, never hinting of one or two extra nights in the tomb, and then especially the nine mentions of *"the third day"*) *seems* to point to a Friday crucifixion and burial, rather than on Wednesday or Thursday. The evidence is admittedly not airtight, however, so if one wishes to hold to the literal *"three days and three nights,"* he can do so, but he should recognize that the other viewpoint is at least equally legitimate.

The essential point, of course, is that the Lord Jesus died for our sins, was buried and rose again. Perhaps God has deliberately left the exact duration a little ambiguous, so that we not judge one another *"in respect of an holyday . . . or of the sabbath days"* (Col. 2:16).

Now, of course, if Christ's *"three days and three nights"* can be understood idiomatically, so can those of Jonah. Jonah's body need not have been in the belly of the great fish for three 24-hour days, though it must at least have been there for one entire day and night and parts of two others. The straightforward simile of Matthew 12:40 would surely indicate this. This further indicates that Jonah's travel time in the fish, from the Tarshish ship somewhere in the open sea back to an undesignated shore en route to Nineveh could have been somewhat less than 72 hours, but at least about 30 hours.

That was quite a journey, like none before or since, the first stage by Phoenician merchant ship, the second by chartered whale line! And it was far from over yet.

But first we need to look in some detail at Jonah's interim stopover in the bottom of the sea and then time spent in hades itself.

FIVE

JONAH'S PRAYER IN HELL

The second chapter of the Book of Jonah is surely the most amazing portion of this uniquely remarkable book. It was necessary to digress from the narrative briefly because of the problem of the three days and nights, the period spent in the body of the whale by Jonah and later appropriated by Christ as a typological prediction of the period that His human body would spend dead in the tomb. But now we must return to the experiences of Jonah himself.

It now appears almost certain that Jonah, like Christ, actually died, drowned in the billowing sea when the sailors cast him overboard to quiet the raging storm. Recall again the words of Christ, uttered in answer to the demand of the scribes and Pharisees for a miraculous sign.

> *But he answered and said unto them, An evil and adulterous generation seeketh after a sign; and there shall no sign*

be given to it, but the sign of the prophet Jonas: For as Jonas was three days and three nights in the whale's belly; so shall the Son of man be three days and three nights in the heart of the earth (Matt. 12:39–40).

The Lord Jesus here acknowledged that Jonah had been a real prophet and that his experience had indeed been a "sign," or miracle, and also that He himself would undergo the same experience as that of Jonah, and that this would be the one great miraculous sign that He was indeed who and what He claimed. He obviously, in retrospect, was referring to His own coming death and resurrection, which would demonstrate once and for all time His power as our Creator, the one true God of both death and life.

Note, however, that His sleeping body spent the time in the garden tomb carved out and fitted for Him by Joseph of Arimathea, not *"in the heart of the earth."* His body rested in the tomb, of course, but His soul/spirit *"went and preached unto the spirits in prison"* (1 Pet. 3:19). That is, *"quickened by the Spirit"* (1 Pet. 3:18), He descended deep into the great pit in the center of the earth known as hades (or sheol in the Old Testament) where the spirits of the dead are incarcerated. *Hades* (Greek) and *sheol* (Hebrew) are both translated as "hell" in the King James Bible and a number of other Bibles, even though it is only a temporary hell; the ultimate lake of fire awaits activation at the second coming of Christ.

The Bible indicates that sheol or hades is a great abyss deep in the heart of the earth. Before Christ came, the spirits of all who died descended into this pit, whether they were saved or unsaved. Christ indicated, however, that there was *"a great gulf fixed "* which separated the spirits of the saved and unsaved from each other (Luke 16:26).

Although geophysicists have never detected the existence of such a pit, they certainly have not disproved its existence, and the Bible often refers to it. Its inhabitants are not in their physical bodies, of course, and we have no way of measuring the "space" required by a spirit, so whether scientists can locate it or not is irrelevant. It is sometimes referred to as *"the nether parts of the earth"* (e.g., Ezek. 31:18; 32:18), where the real definition of the Hebrew word for "nether" is "lowermost." It is translated *"lowest"* in Psalm 86:13. *"For great is thy mercy toward me: and thou hast delivered my soul from the lowest hell."*

When the Lord Jesus left His body in Joseph's tomb, in His Spirit, He *"preached "* [that is, "proclaimed"] His victory on the cross to the unsaved *"spirits in prison"* who had perished in the great flood that destroyed all these rebels against God in the days of Noah (see 1 Pet. 3:18–22).

Although Christ had descended into hell, He would not stay there very long. As predicted through the psalmist David and then later preached by Peter and Paul, He would say of His Father: *"For thou wilt not leave my soul in hell* [that is, sheol]; *neither wilt thou suffer thine Holy One to see corruption* [through bodily decay by a long stay in the tomb]" (Ps. 16:10; Acts 2:27; see also Acts 13:35).

The same had been true of Jonah, whose experience made him such a remarkable type of Christ. His spirit was in *"the belly of hell"* (Jon. 2:2), while his body was for a brief period *"in the belly of the fish"* (Jon. 1:17). As noted in the preceding chapter, that period was, at least in a metaphorical sense, *"three days and three nights,"* although this did not necessarily mean a full 72 hours.

JONAH 2:1–2

> *Then Jonah prayed unto the LORD his God out of the fish's belly.*
>
> *And said, I cried by reason of mine affliction unto the LORD, and he heard me; out of the belly of hell cried I, and thou heardest my voice.*

It is noteworthy that Jonah prayed twice, once in the belly of hell, once in the belly of the fish. These do not refer to the same prayer. In fact, two different Hebrew words are used for "belly."

When speaking of the fish's belly, the word *meah* was used, referring to any of the actual insides of the great fish. When referring to the belly of hell, however, the word was *beten*, a word which also means "womb" and, in fact, is translated "womb" more often than "belly." This seems to suggest that, when Jonah later emerged from the fish, it was sort of like a birth. In fact, Jonah was indeed a different man when he came forth from the great fish than when he was fleeing to Tarshish.

Chapter 2 of the Book of Jonah evidently consists mainly of the prayer he prayed while in sheol, although various liberal theologians have said that this chapter was simply a psalm, some later writer who composed it using various verses and thoughts extracted out of the Book of Psalms. If we take it at face value, however, it is clearly what Jonah prayed while his spirit was in sheol, then recalled later when his spirit returned to his dead body in the belly of the great fish. He probably had died by drowning; his body had been swallowed by the whale while his soul/spirit went down to sheol. The fact that some of the thoughts and phrases in Jonah's prayer are similar to some in the Psalms is a testimony to Jonah's familiarity with the Scriptures, especially the Book of Psalms. For example, compare Jonah 2:2 with Psalm 40:1–2, and 120:1.

It is fascinating to think about what he might have heard and seen while he was there. There were bound to be multitudes of people already there — all those who died in the global flood plus the millions who had died since that time. The prophet Ezekiel later was given a remarkable vision of this temporary hell and its inhabitants.

Speaking of the Assyrians and their king, who had by that time enslaved the people of Israel and were soon destined to be destroyed themselves, Ezekiel said, *"For they are all delivered unto death, to the nether parts of the earth, in the midst of the children of men, with them that go down to the pit. . . . I made the nations to shake at the sound of his fall, when I cast him down to hell with them that descend into the pit"* (Ezek. 31:14–16).

Ezekiel in his vision of hell was later also enabled to see *"Pharaoh and all his multitude,"* *"Asshur . . . and all her company,"* *"Elam and all her multitude,"* *"Meshech, Tubal, and all her multitude,"* *"Edom, her kings, and all her princes,"* *"the princes of the north, all of*

While Jonah's soul/spirit was praying in hell (note Jon. 2:2), his body, wrapped in seaweeds, was shortly to be swallowed up by a divinely prepared and directed fish, probably a great sperm whale. There he remained, spirit-soul-body all reunited after God answered his prayer in hell and raised him from death.

them, and all the Zidonians" — representatives of all three branches of Noah's family (Ezek. 31:18; 32:22, 24, 26, 29, 30), all bound in sheol.

Ezekiel did not speak about the gulf between the saved and unsaved which Christ later mentioned (Luke 16:26), but there is no doubt that there were many on the side of the lost, and only a few in the side which Christ called *"Abraham's bosom,"* seemingly centered around *"Father Abraham,"* said later by the apostle Paul to be not only the father of God's chosen people Israel but also all *"they which are of faith, the same are the children of Abraham"* (Gal. 3:7). Sadly, the great majority of the pagan world had been given up by God and probably most individual Israelites as well, for as Jesus pointed out: *"Narrow is the way, which leadeth unto life, and few there be that find it"* (Matt. 7:14).

The relative few that were with Father Abraham were released from the prison house of sheol by Christ when He came there. The price of their redemption had just been paid in full on the cross, and Christ had come to set them free! *"When he ascended up on high, he led captivity captive"* (Eph. 4:8). And ever since that glorious day, whenever a saved man or woman dies, the spirit no longer has to be confined for a time in hades, but can immediately *"depart . . . to be with Christ; which is far better"* (Phil. 1:23). *"To be absent from the body,"* for the true Christian believer, is *"to be present with the Lord"* (2 Cor. 5:8).

Now whether Jonah saw Abraham or Asshur or any of the others there, saved or lost, his account does not say. Probably he was not interested at all in others who were there; his one concern was to get out of there, and get back to where he could serve the

Lord once again, having definitely repented of his rebellion and his attempt to escape God and His will.

In fact, as we surmised in the previous chapter, his repentance may well have led to his decision to leave the ship and trust God to save him and somehow get him back toward Nineveh, unaware of the unique method of transportation the Lord would employ.

Verse 1 of this chapter tells us of his prayer while conscious in the belly of the whale, having returned to life and entered back into his body. He then recounted his amazing experiences as he prayed, especially recalling his prayer and promise which he made while far down in sheol.

One wonders, incidentally, if others pray after they have gone to sheol (or, for that matter, if those who are with Christ in paradise still pray). We do have the account Christ has given us of the unsaved rich man in hell praying, not for his own restoration, but for someone to go and witness to his family. Significantly, however, he only prayed to Abraham, not to God (see Luke 16:22–31).

Obviously, there is very little to go on here, but what hints we have might suggest that, if there *are* prayers after death, the great burden of those prayers might be for those still on earth — either for them to escape the torments of hell or to enjoy the blessings of paradise. There is that intriguing passage in Hebrews 12:1, telling us that we are *"compassed about,"* like athletes being observed by spectators in a stadium, by a *"great cloud of witnesses"* observing how we run the race here on earth following the wonderful tabulation in Hebrews 11 of heroes of earlier generations who faithfully and successfully had finished *their* race.

We can't help but wonder also whether the few who were restored to life after dying (e.g., Lazarus, Tabitha) had any such encounters. There are eight of these temporary restorations to life recorded in the Bible, but not one of them, as far as the record goes at least, ever said anything about his or her experiences in either hades or paradise. Probably, as Paul said after his own brief view of paradise, they had *"heard unspeakable words, which it is not lawful for a man to utter"* (2 Cor. 12:4). We simply have to wait until we get there ourselves. In the meantime, we have all we need to know for now, in the Holy Scriptures, and we would do well not to put too much credence in the assertions of certain people today who claim to have had firsthand visions of heaven or hell. What God wants us to know is in the Bible, and that's enough for now.

Jonah was unique, of course. He apparently did die, presumably by drowning, and then spent some time in sheol, later being restored to life and able to tell us at least about his prayer while there.

His unique experience made him a beautiful type of Christ, but only in measure, of course. Although Jonah died and rose again, he eventually died again, returning to sheol until that wonderful day when Christ would come to take the spirits of himself and the others who had died in faith to heaven with Him to await the true and permanent resurrection day.

There is one other very intriguing insight Jonah (as well as Christ in His narrative of Lazarus the beggar, in Luke 16) has given us. That is, while the physical body lies dead, the spiritual body still can exercise most of the physical functions of that body.

That is, Jonah could still think and speak while in sheol, composing and crying out his prayer (he mentions his "voice," for example in verse 2). Similarly in Christ's account of the experience of the rich man in hell (that is, hades, the temporary hell), he is said to have requested *"water"* to *"cool my tongue; for I am tormented in this flame"* (Luke 16:24).

However, the account also says plainly that the rich man had *"died, and was buried "* (Luke 16:22). How could a dead and buried body feel a flame and beg water to cool his tongue?

Somehow, the spirit/soul complex in our physical bodies survives the death of our body, but does not remain disembodied. As Paul wrote concerning Christians who die:

> *If our earthly house of this tabernacle were dissolved, we have a building of God, an house not made with hands, eternal in the heavens. For in this we groan, earnestly desiring to be clothed upon with our house which is from heaven* (2 Cor. 5:1–2).

There is much that we do not understand. How can a "bodyless" spirit see and hear and speak and feel? We just need to remember that God is the *Creator*! He designed and created our amazingly complex present physical bodies. We can safely assume He is capable of creating spiritual bodies, capable of speaking and hearing, and of being recognized as somehow like our present bodies, yet still made of intangible materials and forces which are not subject to our present physiological constraints. These are not to be our final, permanent resurrection bodies, but will certainly suffice for whatever time duration may occur before the return of Christ and the glorious resurrection day.

Our discussion has carried us into areas even more mysterious than the question of how Jonah could be swallowed by a whale and survive. But there are certain often-asked questions (will we know each other after death? do people still pray in heaven? etc.) which seem naturally to surface when we think about Jonah praying in sheol — and that is what his record says he did! But now we need to look at his actual prayer.

JONAH 2:3–4

> *For thou hadst cast me into the deep, in the midst of the seas; and the floods compassed me about: all thy billows and thy waves passed over me.*
>
> *Then I said, I am cast out of thy sight; yet I will look again toward thy holy temple.*

This is Jonah's prayer while in sheol, rehearsed again after he came to life again in the fish's belly. He had first acknowledged that the Lord had heard his prayer (verse 2), but now he was remembering what he had actually prayed down there. He noted in his prayer that it was God who had cast him into the deep; yet he was well aware that the mariners had done this, and had done it only at his own insistence.

This fact reinforces the previous implication that God must have spoken to Jonah at the height of the terrible storm, assuring him that, if he left the ship, God would somehow transport him back to shore and on toward Nineveh. Thus it was really God who had sent him down into the ocean.

As he plunged deeper into the waters, *"the floods"* surrounded him. Actually, there are over ten different Hebrew words translated "flood" in the Bible. The one used here seems primarily to refer to a flooding river. Jonah seemed to feel that it was like many great rivers pouring their waters over him all at once. The storm, in fact, had seemed like that, with violent winds and waves continually changing directions and preventing any attempts to control and steer the ship.

But then the surface billows and waves gradually attenuated as he continued to sink down. Jonah was bound to be trying to hold his breath and probably beginning to be concerned that, although the Lord in effect had cast him into the deep, yet now he (Jonah) seemed to have been cast out of God's sight altogether. Jonah briefly wondered whether he had made a dreadful mistake in persuading the seamen to cast him overboard. Note the similarity of verse 3 to Psalm 42:7.

Yet his faith quickly returned, even as he felt himself drowning. *"I will look again toward thy holy temple,"* he assured himself and the Lord, as he tried to pray even in dying.

Although his home had been in Zebulon, many miles north of Jerusalem and the holy temple, his heart was there at the temple. After all, he was a true prophet of God and had probably managed at least occasionally to worship in the temple and offer sacrifices there. Like Daniel (Dan. 6:10), he surely had customarily prayed even at home facing toward Jerusalem and its temple. Now he thought of this even as he was dying, and in faith believed that the Lord would indeed save him and one day bring him back to the temple.

JONAH 2:5–6

> *The waters compassed me about, even to the soul: the depth closed me round about, the weeds were wrapped about my head.*
>
> *I went down to the bottom of the mountains; the earth with her bars was about me for ever: yet hast thou brought up my life from corruption, O LORD my God.*

Finally the deep waters so completely enclosed him that his soul could no longer sustain his body, and he died. He remembered going down, down, even to the bottom of the mountains, where the lush sea weeds on the ocean floor wrapped around his head.

It is an interesting sidelight that Jonah had descended down even to *"the bottom of the mountains."* So far as we know, the people of Jonah's day had no way of exploring the floor of the oceans, so did not know that the coastal mountain ranges extended below the adjacent ground level and on down to the bottom of the sea. Yet Jonah could actually see that this was the case, and so mentioned it even in his prayer.

Then, as Jonah's soul descended into the great pit sheol, in the heart of the earth, it seemed to Jonah that, with great depths of earth surrounding him on all sides, there could be no way out. It was like the earth itself had great bars completely enclosing the pit, and he was doomed to stay there forever.

The Bible frequently mentions bars in houses or gates or other structures, installed for strength and security. But now it seems that the earth's interior had great bars surrounding this prison-house of souls.

No one could get past those bars on *"the gates of hell"* (Matt. 16:18), except the one who had built them there. God could take Jonah back through them, just as Christ some 800 years later would open them for the souls of all who had died in faith, taking them with Him back to *"paradise"* in *"the third heaven"* (2 Cor. 12:2, 4). He had told the dying, but believing, thief on the cross: *"To day shalt thou be with me in paradise"* (Luke 23:43).

And He did just that, after proclaiming His victory to all the fallen angels and lost souls, then releasing all the souls of those who had believed in God's promises (including the dying thief to whom He had spoken on the cross). *"When He ascended up on high, He led captivity captive"* (Eph. 4:8), *"proclaiming liberty to the captives, and the opening of the prison to them that are bound"* (Isa. 61:1).

Jonah no doubt would also have been in that company of freed captives, for (although we have no record of his eventual death) he did eventually die again. In fact there have been two competing traditional grave sites for Jonah — one in his home town of Gath-sepher, one in Nineveh, where he preached so successfully.

Jonah, as the pre-ordained type of Christ, had traveled down there briefly once before, while his body was resting in the whale's belly (analogous to the body of the Lord Jesus resting in the grave), but he prayed earnestly and the Lord brought him back. Then, as he returned to consciousness in his physical body, he prayed with deep thankfulness: *"Yet hast thou brought up my life from corruption* [the Hebrew for "corruption" can also mean "a pit" and possibly here refers to the great pit sheol], *O LORD my God."*

Jonah's language here is similar to David's, when he was prophesying Christ's future resurrection: *"For thou wilt not leave my soul in hell; neither wilt thou suffer thine Holy One to see corruption"* (Ps. 16:10). This verse was quoted by Peter and applied to Christ in his key sermon on the day of Pentecost (Acts 2:27).

JONAH 2:7–9

When my soul fainted within me I remembered the LORD: and my prayer came in unto thee, into thine holy temple.

They that observe lying vanities forsake their own mercy.

But I will sacrifice unto thee with the voice of thanksgiving; I will pay that that I have vowed. Salvation is of the LORD.

In these verses, Jonah is completing His prayer of remembrance, repentance, and thanksgiving after the Lord had brought his soul back from sheol and back to consciousness in his physical body, which had been resting in death in the belly of the great fish. This fish, which has been assumed here to be something like the great sperm whale, had presumably swallowed Jonah near the sea floor, about the time he lost consciousness and died.

He is still recalling the urgent prayer he prayed just after he died (implied here by the reference to his soul fainting) when he realized he was in hell. He then *"remembered the LORD"* and immediately began praying, confident that God would hear him in heaven — not just in the Jerusalem temple, but in the heavenly temple after which the earthly temple had been patterned (note Heb. 8:5; Ps. 11:4). Note also how his words here are reminiscent of Psalm 18:6.

As he prayed, he recalled how foolish he had been in thinking he could escape the God of heaven and earth by trusting in a group of pagan mariners to take him far away from both Israel and Nineveh. These men all served various *"lying vanities"* — that is, "worthless idols" — as did the Assyrians to whom the Lord had sent him to preach. The impotence of these gods had been made abundantly clear when they could not answer the prayers of the sailors who had called on them to calm the terrible storm.

Jonah in effect had himself trusted these *"lying vanities,"* and now was deeply ashamed and repentant. He had forsaken the God who not only was omnipotent but also full of mercy. He had even demonstrated His nature of mercy by sending Jonah to preach to the Ninevites, and Jonah had forsaken Him and His mercy by running away.

But Jonah now called on that mercy once again, promising to offer sacrifices — even himself as a living sacrifice — with true thanksgiving for the privilege of knowing and serving such a God, evidently solemnly vowing this time to carry out the mission to Nineveh that God had assigned to him.

Then he concluded his prayer with the great affirmation that *"Salvation is of the LORD."* That saving Lord had saved him from death in the storm, from death by drowning, from death inside a great whale, and — most amazing of all — from eternal death in hell. And, of course, God had been the Savior of His people Israel and could well save even the Assyrians and Phoenicians and any others who would turn to Him from idols.

It is worth noting at least that the Hebrew word for "salvation" here is *Yeshua,* essentially the name "Jesus."

And with this prayer, climaxed by Jonah's recognition and assertion that salvation (whether temporal or eternal, physical or spiritual, earthly or heavenly) can come only from God (through the Lord Jesus, of whom Jonah has been made such a striking type), Jonah's unique ordeal was over. But not his journey!

JONAH 2:10

And the LORD spake unto the fish, and it vomited out Jonah upon the dry land.

The impression given here by Jonah's record is that the whale deposited him on the shore almost as soon as he had finished his prayer. Most of the three days and three nights (or whatever the exact duration was) may have been spent in sheol as far as Jonah's soul was concerned. The body, of course, was in the whale's belly all that time. Then when Jonah's soul/spirit returned to his body, he probably immediately began to pour forth his prayer of thanksgiving. Although the written prayer which Jonah later wrote down may have been only a summary of his whole prayer, the latter probably did not take much time, and then all of a sudden there he was out on dry land!

One can hardly begin to imagine the complex of feelings that rushed over Jonah at this time. Awe, joy, thankfulness, amazement — no one had ever been through such an experience before, and here he was, alive and well back on dry land. Whatever he may have felt, he was surely not in a rebellious mood any longer. He was fully determined to do whatever God said.

The account does not say where he landed. It may well have been back at Joppa, where he could start over again. Josephus, the Jewish historian, suggests that it may have been on a coast of the Black Sea. The Lord still wanted him to go to Nineveh, and it would be possible for God to direct the whale to the closest point to that city if He so chose.

Wherever that may have been, the journey in the whale from the ship to land occupied three days and three nights at the most. This does not help much, since we do not know how fast the whale could swim or where he took Jonah on board.

In any case, that was certainly the most unusual trip in all the history of ocean travel. The whale no doubt wanted to get rid of the uncomfortable object in its belly as soon as it could, and the language rather graphically suggests its haste to do so when it finally reached God's designated drop-off point, and *"vomited"* Jonah out.

Nevertheless, there he was, safe and sound, and no longer of a mind to run away from God and His Word.

Six

That Great City, Nineveh

Although Jonah had been brought back to land by the whale, it would still be a long journey to get to Nineveh. Since the account does not say where he landed, we don't know exactly how far, but it would surely be a minimum of 400 miles. Neither does the account say whether he would have a horse or camel or, more likely, have to travel on foot.

Nineveh was on the eastern bank of the Tigris River, not too far down from its source on Mount Ararat, and near the modern city of Mosul in northern Iraq. If perchance Josephus was right in saying the whale discharged Jonah on a shore of the Black Sea, it turns out that the shortest distance to Nineveh would be across the rugged Anatolian plateau. Perhaps a crossing route of some kind had been developed by early caravans or other travelers. In any case, it would still be a difficult and possibly dangerous trip that would take a good amount of time.

Nevertheless, after his terrifying experience in the storm, the sea, the whale, and even in hell, Jonah was now willing to go to

Nineveh. As confirmation of his mission, however, the Lord spoke to him again at this point.

JONAH 3:1–2

> *And the word of the LORD came unto Jonah the second time, saying,*
>
> *Arise, go unto Nineveh, that great city, and preach unto it the preaching that I bid thee.*

Nineveh was, indeed, a great city, a wicked city, and a very ancient city. It is gone now, of course, and for centuries almost forgotten, except for the records in the Bible. In fact, some skeptics had even denied there ever was such a city until it was excavated in the mid-19th century by A.H. Layard and others. Thousands of clay tablets were found there, dealing with a wide range of subjects, from religious legends to commercial transactions, as well as a somewhat distorted record of early history, including the Great Flood.

We know from its mention in the Table of Nations (Gen. 10:11) that Nineveh was one of the earliest cities built in the post-Flood world. Most Old Testament authorities believe that Genesis 10:11–12, should read: *"Out of that land* [that is, Babel] *he* [Nimrod] *went forth to Asshur, and builded Nineveh, and the city Rehoboth, and Calah. And Resen between Nineveh and Calah: the same is a great city."*

That is, the nation of Assyria had actually been founded by Asshur, second son of Shem, probably after the confusion of tongues and scattering of the clans at Babel by God. Nimrod later came and founded Nineveh. Another possibility, though not mentioned specifically in the Bible, is that Asshur never did settle in Babel and thus did not take part in Nimrod's rebellion there. Shem, his father, probably stayed near Noah, and tried to teach his own sons about the God of his father. If perchance Asshur had resisted Nimrod's apostasy, it would not be surprising if Nimrod decided to compete with Asshur, and built Nineveh as his own center of military operations in Assyria. Nineveh is apparently named after Ninus, supposedly the same as Nimrod.

This latter is pure speculation, of course, but history does show that the Babylonians and Assyrians had been fighting each other from their very beginnings. By the time of Jonah, many dynasties had come and gone. Whatever commitment the first Assyrians under Asshur may have had to the true God had been long forgotten by Jonah's time. Their kings and the people in general had become extremely licentious and cruel, especially in their devotion to Ishtar, the Babylonian goddess of fertility and war, but they worshiped various other gods as well.

They were notoriously cruel to their enemies when they conquered them, and they were becoming more aggressive and powerful all the time. The prophet Hosea was a younger contemporary of Jonah, and his prophecies had begun to warn Israel that, unless they repented, the Israelites were going to end up conquered by these ungodly Assyrians (see Hos. 8:9; 11:5; etc.). As a result, Jonah had developed a deep fear and hatred of the whole nation of Assyria and would have been happy to see her destroyed altogether.

Nineveh was not the Assyrian capital until about Jonah's time, but seems to have become the largest and most wicked of all the Assyrian cities, possibly because of the ongoing influence of Nimrod, its founder. The capital was at that time possibly still at Asshur, as originally established by Asshur himself. As noted previously, however, all of Assyria had become known as *"the land of Nimrod "* (Mic. 5:6).

Thus it is not surprising that Jonah despised Nineveh and the Assyrians and he must have wondered why God wanted him to preach to them instead of some more amenable Gentile nation. Could it be that because of their heritage (Shem and Asshur) God wanted to give them one last chance? Or, more likely, was it to demonstrate that He could save even the worst of men if they would only repent and believe? The apostle Paul, for example, had been the most bitter enemy of Christians until he was converted, but then we remember what God did through him!

Anyway, God still wanted Jonah to go to Nineveh and preach to its people, whether or not he understood why. Furthermore, he was to preach the message that God would give him, not some message of his own devising. That message was certainly going to include a warning of coming judgment, and Jonah was quite agreeable at least to that. Although he had reason to fear that the Ninevites might well respond to such a message with violence against himself, he definitely realized by now that God could protect him, for He had already delivered him from hell itself.

> *So Jonah arose, and went unto Nineveh, according to the word of the LORD. Now Nineveh was an exceeding great city of three days' journey.*
>
> *And Jonah began to enter into the city a day's journey, and he cried, and said, Yet forty days, and Nineveh shall be overthrown.*

For the second time, Jonah tells us that he *"rose up"*: the first time, he *"rose up to flee unto Tarshish"* from the will of God; this second time he *"arose, and went unto Nineveh"* in obedience to the will of God. In both cases, the word *"rose up"* or *"arose"* (same Hebrew word) indicates intensity of determination. Like the son in Christ's parable, when the father told him to work in his vineyard, he first said, *"I will not: but afterward he repented, and went"* (Matt. 21:29).

As noted above, it was quite a journey just to get to Nineveh; then Nineveh itself was a city of *"three days' journey."* The Greek historian Herodotus described a "day's journey" as about 150 stadia, or almost six miles. This would suggest that, at that time, Nineveh was about 18 miles in diameter, with a circumference of about 57 miles. Other writers have suggested a probable circumference of 60 miles. These dimensions are comparable to those of many major modern cities.

On the other hand, the extensive archaeological excavations in the ruins of Nineveh do not indicate a city that large, although it was indeed a very large city for that day and time. When Jonah said it was a city of three days' journey, he could well have implied that it would take three days to cross it while slowing or stopping to preach at many locations along the way.

Another possibility is that, in Jonah's book, the name Nineveh included all its suburban cities — that is, Rehoboth, Resen, and Calah, as listed in Genesis 10:11–12. Calah in particular is said to have been *"a great city."*

As Jonah began to enter into Nineveh's metropolitan area, "a day's journey," he began to preach wherever he was able to get a group together. With his very unwelcome message, he knew he was not likely to be invited to speak in one of the pagan temples of the city, so he initiated the practice of what today we would call "street meetings." He preached loudly (*"cried,"* the account says), so he was evidently able to gather a crowd wherever he preached. Somehow he was able to speak in the Assyrian language. Whether he had studied enough Assyrian to do this, or whether he was an early recipient of a supernatural "gift of tongues," we are not told. But preach he did!

He may well have amplified his preaching beyond what he has said in his book, but the essential theme always was this: *"Yet forty days, and Nineveh shall be overthrown."* He probably also urged the hearers to repent, but he probably had little confidence or desire that they would do so. After all, to them he may have seemed just an itinerant preacher (they may even have thought he was only a typical rabble rouser), so why should they listen to him? It seems strange that the authorities didn't soon have him thrown into prison, or worse.

But listen to him they did! It is just possible that, by the time he reached Nineveh, the populace had heard about the amazing events that had taken place on his way to Tarshish, and so realized that Jonah was, indeed, a man sent to them by God. It may even be that his skin and general appearance looked so unearthly, as a result of his body's sojourn in the whale's belly, that the people stood in awe of him as they watched him preach, and were afraid to interfere with him. Somehow as Jesus said, Jonah *was a sign unto the Ninevites"* (Luke 11:30). In any case, he shouted forth his warnings of imminent doom, and the people began to believe him.

It has also been suggested by many that the superstitious Assyrians had been conditioned to accept a message from heaven by a total eclipse of the sun that had occurred in that part of the world about 768 B.C.

Another suggestion has been that Jonah was believed to be a reincarnation of a legendary man-fish named Yanush (somewhat similar phonetically to Jonah) who in the very early history of Assyria had appeared out of the sea and had taught the Assyrians many things to better their way of life.

Whatever the reasons, real or imagined, for the willingness of the Assyrians to heed Jonah's message, they quickly reported to their king (possibly just the governor of that region), and he immediately commanded the whole city to repent and fast and pray for mercy from God. *"So the people of Nineveh believed God . . . from the greatest of them to the least of them"* (Jon. 3:5).

Jonah told the crowds of those who would listen that God had given the city just 40 days to repent and turn back to the true

Nineveh, *"an exceeding great city of three days journey,"* had an area, with its suburbs, equivalent to that of San Francisco and a large part of the bay area around it (Jon. 3:3).

God. It is worth noting in that connection how often a period of 40 days is mentioned in the Bible, usually as a period either of testing or judgment. That was the period of most intense rain at the time of the Flood (Gen. 7:12), for example, and it was also the period during which the delegates from the tribes spied out the land of Canaan, and then had to wander 40 years in the wilderness because of the *"evil report of the land "*(Num. 13:32) which they brought back to Moses (Num. 14:33–34).

Moses was on the mountain 40 days to receive the law on Sinai (Exod. 24:18), then again a second time (Exod. 34:28) as a result of the tragic affair of Aaron and the golden calf while he was in the mount the first time. It was also 40 days that the Philistine giant Goliath taunted Israel and the men of Saul, until young David accepted the challenge to fight him (1 Sam. 17:16).

Elijah's flight from Jezebel occupied 40 days as he sought God in Mount Horeb (1 Kings 19:8). Ezekiel the prophet, during Judah's Babylonian exile, was told by God to lie on his right side for 40 days, symbolizing the 40 years of continued rebellion of Judah after God had warned them that they also would be sent into captivity as the northern kingdom of Israel had been (Ezek. 4:6; 2 Kings 23:27).

Most significantly of all, 40 days was the period of Christ's testing by Satan near the beginning of His public ministry (Matt. 4:2; Mark 1:13; Luke 4:2). Then, after His death and resurrection, He demonstrated His eternal victory over sin and judgment, *"by many infallible proofs, being seen of them forty days"* (Acts 1:3).

Jonah undoubtedly preached this message of imminent overthrow with great conviction, since Assyria was a dangerous threat to Israel and he truly wanted it to happen. It never occurred to him that such a wicked city as Nineveh could ever repent and that God would then actually delay her destruction for over a hundred years.

But that is what happened!

JONAH 3:5–9

So the people of Nineveh believed God, and proclaimed a fast, and put on sackcloth, from the greatest of them even to the least of them.

For word came unto the king of Nineveh, and he arose from his throne, and he laid his robe from him, and covered him with sackcloth, and sat in ashes.

And he caused it to be proclaimed and published throughout Nineveh by the decree of the king and his nobles, saying, Let neither man nor beast, herd nor flock, taste any thing: let them not feed, nor drink water:

But let man and beast be covered with sackcloth, and cry mightily unto God: yea, let them turn every one from his evil way, and from the violence that is in their hands.

Who can tell if God will turn and repent, and turn away from His fierce anger, that we perish not?

It is almost incredible, but it happened! Instead of rejecting Jonah and probably killing him, as one would have predicted would happen, they believed his message and turned to the true God! There have been a number of great religious revivals in history, but nothing else was ever like this. From the king on his throne down to the lowliest peasant, they *"believed God."*

Many later readers, of course, have found this account itself unbelievable. Secular historians have found no record of such an event in any of the Assyrian monuments or tablets, and we do know that Assyria later became more wicked and cruel than ever.

Some have pointed to a brief period, apparently sometime before Jonah preached there, when the king of Assyria worshiped only the god Nebo, one member of the Assyrian pantheon. Nebo was certainly not Jehovah, however, so this fact has little relevance to Jonah's revival.

The fact that Jonah's revival is mentioned in the Bible is sufficient evidence for us to believe that it really happened. Of course, its factuality was later confirmed by Christ himself, and He would surely know! He said to the people of his own generation, *"The men of Nineveh shall rise in judgment with this generation, and shall condemn it: because they repented at the preaching of Jonas; and, behold, a greater than Jonas is here"* (Matt. 12:41).

If anyone asks why there is no mention of this in the Assyrian tablets, we could answer that they have not found the right tablet yet. Of the thousands of tablets and monuments excavated so far, there are many that have not yet been translated. And there are many more not yet excavated.

There may be another possibility. The ancient kings were notorious for recording in detail their victories and notable achievements, while destroying any records of their failures. They liked to boast of their exploits, not record their defeats. It is quite possible that one of the later kings, after the Assyrians had returned to paganism, decided to destroy any evidence that his people had ever worshiped the God of the despised Hebrews.

And return to paganism they did, with a vengeance! A little over a century later, the prophet Nahum wrote his entire three-chapter book against Nineveh, which by then had long been the capital of the Assyrians, predicting her imminent destruction. His final chapter begins and ends as follows: *"Woe to the bloody city! It is all full of lies and robbery; the prey departeth not. . . . There is no healing of thy bruise; thy wound is grievous: all that hear the bruit of thee shall clap the hands over thee: for upon whom hath not thy wickedness passed continually?"* (Nah. 3:1–19).

The prophet Zephaniah was also, like Nahum, a prophet in Judah. However, he also gave a significant prophetic warning to Assyria: *"And* [the LORD] *will stretch out His hand against the north, and destroy Assyria; and will make Nineveh a desolation, and dry like a wilderness. . . . This is the rejoicing city that dwelt carelessly, that said in her heart, I am, and there is none beside me: how is she become a desolation, a place for beasts to lie down in! every one that passeth by her shall hiss, and wag his hand "* (Zeph. 2:13–15).

These prophecies have been quite literally fulfilled. Assyria was a great and powerful empire, and Nineveh was a great city, but God finally determined that her iniquity, like that of the Amorites, was full (note Gen. 15:16) and her appointed time was finished (Nah. 3:7).

But there was a brief time there when Assyria turned to God, and His destructive judgment was postponed. Instead of the 40 days prophesied by Jonah, Nineveh was given another 100 years or more, finally coming to her end at the famous battle of

Carchemish, 605 B.C. (Nineveh herself had been defeated in 612 B.C.) The combined forces of the Medes, Babylonians, and Scythians constituted the vehicle that God used to judge and destroy the mighty Assyrian empire. A remnant did escape to the mountains of what is now Kurdistan, and these somehow eventually professed Christianity, continuing to exist today in the Assyrian Christian Church, centered in northern Iraq.

Just how deep and genuine the revival under Jonah may have been is a question, of course. It was certainly sincere, resulting in a nationwide fast and repentance, led by the king and his nobles. The king, who had apparently never been confronted personally by Jonah, nevertheless had heard enough about him and his preaching to perceive that his message really came from the God of creation. He issued a proclamation that *"every one"* should *"turn . . . from his evil way, and from . . . violence"* and that *"man and beast be covered with sackcloth"* and then *"cry mightily unto God."*

What a sight and sound that must have been! Imagine all the citizens — and even the animals — clothed in sackcloth (a coarse-textured dark-colored cloth made of goat or camel hair) and praying loudly to Jonah's God, asking Him to spare the city.

The Lord *did* hear and spare the city. But they could hardly have learned much about God and His salvation just from Jonah's warning of judgment. They certainly did not become proselytes to the whole Israelite religious system, so how much they grasped about salvation or the other great truths implicit in the worship of Jehovah is very doubtful.

But at least *that* generation was spared immediate physical death, and we can just possibly hope to see at least some of them in heaven. Whatever the revival amounted to, however, it probably didn't survive beyond that current generation. It wasn't long before the younger generations were back to their same old wicked ways, and Jonah's prediction (except the timing) would eventually come to pass anyway.

Jonah, of course, did not want the delay. In fact, the Assyrians would eventually conquer his own country because of *their* wickedness and take them away into captive exile, probably not too many years (we don't know just how many) after Jonah died.

In any case, God did lengthen the days of Nineveh and Assyria 100 or more years because of their prayers of repentance, no matter how imperfect these prayers may have been. He is a gracious and merciful God.

JONAH 3:10

And God saw their works, that they turned from their evil way; and God repented of the evil, that he had said that he would do unto them; and he did it not.

Except for one point, we have already discussed the action described in this verse.

That point is the question of God's "repentance." It is true that *"the Strength of Israel will not lie nor repent: for he is not a man, that he should repent"* (1 Sam. 15:29).

Yet this verse, as well as others (e.g., 1 Sam. 15:11; Gen. 6:7), indicates that He *does* repent on occasion. This cannot really be a contradiction, of course, although superficially it might appear to be one.

We need to look at it something like this. God might "appear" to repent sometimes, but this is only because He cannot *really* repent. *"He cannot deny himself"* (2 Tim. 2:13).

He has promised to forgive when people truly repent and believe. That is, He cannot repent of His promise to repent when people repent! So when the people of Nineveh all repented and believed God, He fulfilled His implied promise to repent [the word means essentially to "change one's mind"] of the destruction He had planned for them if they did not.

But this decision of the Lord did not resonate well with Jonah. He had predicted their destruction within 40 days from the time he started preaching, and *that* was what he wanted to happen.

SEVEN

THE COMPASSIONATE GOD

Jonah had willingly, at the possible risk of life and limb, preached about God's wrath and imminent judgment to the pagan wicked men of Nineveh. Apparently, he was convinced that God would protect him as he preached and then God would indeed visit the city with some form of cataclysmic destruction. This would have eliminated the very real threat to Israel represented by an aggressively belligerent Assyria, and that's exactly what Jonah wanted and expected to happen.

But God had other plans, for reasons unknown to Jonah or even to us 25 centuries later. We have speculated a bit as to why God singled out Assyria (instead of Egypt or Syria or Babylonia, or one of Israel's numerous other enemies) to favor in this way, but we really don't know *why*. He did, however, and we can be thankful (as Jonah should have been) that our God is *"merciful and gracious, slow to anger, and plenteous in mercy"* (Ps. 103:8).

Jonah not only realized this, but was actually fearful that God *would* be merciful to the Ninevites. This was *not* what *he* wanted!

JONAH 4:1–2

> *But it displeased Jonah exceedingly, and he was very angry.*
>
> *And he prayed unto the LORD, and said, I pray thee, O LORD, was not this my saying when I was yet in my country? Therefore I fled before unto Tarshish: for I knew that thou art a gracious God, and merciful, slow to anger, and of great kindness, and repentest thee of the evil.*

Jonah knew much about God's mercy, based on his own experience in Israel. He had been a prophet in Israel during the long reign of King Jeroboam II, who *"did that which was evil in the sight of the LORD"* (2 Kings 14:24). Despite that, God used Jeroboam to save Israel from her enemies and to recover some of the territories taken away from her earlier by Syria. In fact, Jonah himself had prophesied this. Jeroboam had *"restored the coast of Israel from the entering of Hamath unto the sea of the plain, according to the word of the LORD God of Israel, which He spake by the hand of His servant Jonah, the son of Amittai, the prophet, which was of Gath-hepher"* (2 Kings 14:25).

Hamath was a major Syrian city well north of Damascus, so the recovered territories included the Phoenician cities as well as these major Syrian cities. All of this had once been part of the Davidic/Solomonic empire, but apparently had been taken by Syria until Jeroboam was able to recover them. To some degree, Jeroboam was successful in accomplishing this because of the pressure Assyria was exerting on Syria at the time. In a sense, Assyria had been assisting Israel, even though her ultimate plans included taking over all of Israel as well.

Perhaps Jonah was fearful that God was about to favor Assyria, in spite of her dismal and cruel history. He knew that Israel also had departed far from God, even during the prosperous times accompanying Jeroboam's reign. Yet God was still favoring Israel, *"For the LORD saw the affliction of Israel, that it was very bitter. . . . And the LORD said not that he would blot out the name of Israel from under heaven: but he saved them by the hand of Jeroboam the son of Joash"* (2 Kings 14:26–27).

Could it be, Jonah may have wondered, whether, if God was still sparing apostate Israel and even prospering them under such a wicked king as Jeroboam II, He was not thinking of promoting the terrible Assyrian nation in like manner as He had done for Israel — especially now that they seemed to be repentant of their evil ways? It is interesting that Joel, prophesying in Judah probably a good numbers of years later, seems to quote from Jonah when he speaks of God's "repenting" of evil He had threatened (see Joel 2:13).

Yet, how could that really be, when Assyria was so unspeakably vile, worse than any of the other nations? Among other atrocities, they boasted that when they would finally subdue a hostile city that had resisted their takeover, they not only would burn the city, but also mutilate all the male citizens (cutting off their hands and ears and gouging out their eyes), then pile them all in a great heap to die in the sun. The children would all be burnt alive at the stake and the city's governor would be carried off to Assyria to be flayed alive before the Assyrian king. Their military strategy was pure terrorism, instilling such fear in their potential victims as to encourage immediate surrender.

Jonah had good reason to fear what the Assyrians would do to his own nation and its people when their turn came. It was hard for him to entertain the thought that, even after God had threatened to destroy them because of their wickedness, they would now escape because of their apparent repentance. How could he know whether the change was real and would last?

As it turned out, in fact, the change did *not* last long. Although there is no extra-biblical record of the Ninevite revival, we can assume it was real and lasting during that particular generation; Christ seemed to imply that. Although Jonah was wrong in his unforgiving attitude, his concern was understandable in view of Assyrian history, before and after.

JONAH 4:3-4

> *Therefore now, O LORD, take, I beseech thee, my life*
> *from me; for it is better for me to die than to live.*
> *Then said the LORD, Doest thou well to be angry?*

Jonah certainly knew that his life was in the Lord's hand. He had delivered him from hell itself, as well as from drowning and from being swallowed by a whale, and now from the possible fury of the Assyrians when he began preaching imminent judgment to them.

He had wanted God to destroy those wicked and cruelly vindictive people and had no idea that they would actually repent and turn to God as a result of his preaching. But now that they had, it seemed that God might spare them after all. They might even fare better at the hand of God in the future than his own apostate and corrupt nation, and he did not relish that thought at all.

In fact, he became so angry that he would rather die than see anything like that come to pass. If he had ever feared death, he did not now, for he had been there and back. Spiritual existence in hades, presumably in that section called "Abraham's bosom" by Christ, would be better than physical life in a world dominated by the hated Assyrians. With his prophetic insight, perhaps he could even foresee the time in the not-too-distant future when these Assyrians would invade and desecrate his homeland, carrying his people away from their homes and to an unknown fate far in the north.

Therefore, he begged the Lord to let him die now instead, this time not to return. The Lord, however, wanted Jonah to continue his prophetic ministry on earth, so in a mild and loving rebuke, He simply asked him, *"Doest thou well to be angry?"* Jonah should have been overjoyed at the amazing response of the Ninevites! God was clearly working in their midst, at least for a time, and surely Jonah could trust *"the Judge of all the earth"* to *"do right"* (Gen. 18:25).

Perhaps, as suggested above, Jonah had more faith in the Assyrians to do evil than in God to do right. He may have felt their repentance was only superficial and temporary, and they would soon return to their evil ways, especially in the next generation or so. And he would have been right, if that was what he was thinking.

Nevertheless, he should have been thrilled and happy at the conversion of at least that one generation, especially since the Lord had used his own preaching to bring it about.

JONAH 4:5–7

> *So Jonah went out of the city, and sat on the east side of the city, and there made him a booth, and sat under it in the shadow, till he might see what would become of the city.*
>
> *And the LORD God prepared a gourd, and made it to come up over Jonah, that it might be a shadow over his head, to deliver him from his grief. So Jonah was exceeding glad of the gourd.*
>
> *But God prepared a worm when the morning rose the next day, and it smote the gourd that it withered.*

Apparently Jonah still was hoping that God might yet carry out His original threat to overthrow Nineveh in 40 days (Jon. 3:4), so he decided to wait and see. Maybe this city-wide fast and supposed repentance was only superficial; the 40 days were not yet past, so he would at least stay that long.

Just in case that would happen, Jonah did not want to be *in* the city, of course, so he decided to set up a sort of camp *outside* the city. He built a fairly substantial structure in which to wait. The word translated "booth" is often rendered "pavilion" or even "tabernacle," so it seems Jonah was prepared to wait several days.

He chose the east side of the city, presumably because the Tigris River was on the west. It evidently was summertime, or at least a very hot spell, so Jonah sat in the shadow cast by his booth, hoping to be comfortable while he waited. His bleached skin was no doubt painfully sensitive to the sun.

However, this did not help much, so God graciously *"prepared"* a gourd to grow rapidly to provide additional shade. Instead of punishing him for his attitude toward God's change of plans toward Nineveh, God wanted simply to instruct Jonah about His reason for doing so. He loved and wanted to continue to use His prophet, as Israel still urgently needed his message. God could well understand Jonah's fear of the Assyrians, and had already been amazingly patient with him because of his zeal for Israel and God's righteousness and justice. But Jonah still needed to gain a deeper understanding of God's love and grace, as well as His plans for His entire creation, not just Israel.

The gourd (Hebrew *qiyqalown*) is apparently hard to identify, but scholars say that its Hebrew name is similar to an Egyptian name for the castor oil plant. That seems as good a guess as any — unless, that is, it was a special plant created for this one occasion, like the great fish that God prepared to receive and transport Jonah.

In fact, it is interesting that, in this very short Book of Jonah, the word *"prepared"* is used four times to tell us about special acts of God. First, God *"prepared a great fish,"* then He *"prepared a gourd,"* next He *"prepared a worm,"* and finally God *"prepared a vehement east wind"* (Jon. 1:17; 4:6, 7, 8), all for special purposes related to Jonah's calling and ministry.

If the gourd was a castor oil plant, as many believe, this is a plant that does grow rapidly and does have a very large leaf on each branch. These leaves would indeed provide additional shade for Jonah. Whether it would grow this rapidly in one night, however, is very doubtful. More likely it was a miracle plant, and it made Jonah *"exceeding glad."* The same word, incidentally, had been used by Jonah when he described himself as *"exceedingly displeased"* at God's decision to spare Nineveh (Jon. 4:1). Jonah was subject to intensity of feeling, whether of gladness or sadness. In fact, the same Hebrew word was also used to describe Nineveh as a *"great city,"* the fish as a *"great fish,"* and the storm as a *"great tempest"* (Jon. 1:2; 1:17; 1:12). The Hebrew word was *gadowl,* and Jonah apparently liked to use it. For that matter, all his experiences were so out of the ordinary as to require superlatives to describe them!

God saw to it, however, that Jonah's glad appreciation of the shade from the gourd plant lasted only one day, for He sent a special worm to destroy its roots and cause it to wither away in that one day. The castor oil plant is said to both grow quickly and deteriorate quickly, but again this seems to have been a miraculously endowed worm, to do it *this* fast! God had a special lesson for His prophet to learn.

The worm was distinctive in another sense as well, although this could hardly have been obvious to Jonah himself at that time. It was known as the "scarlet worm" (Hebrew *towla*), as being the source of the red fluid used in those days to produce beautiful scarlet and crimson cloth. In fact, the same word was actually translated "crimson" in Isaiah 1:18, speaking of sins being *"red like crimson."*

The strikingly significant thing about this word is that it is used prophetically as applied to Christ on the cross in the marvelous 22nd Psalm. There he says, *"But I am a worm"* (Ps. 22:6). Not just any worm, but the *scarlet* worm, whose blood-red fluid emerging from the body of the female worm as she dies in giving birth to her young speaks eloquently of the shed blood of the Lord Jesus as *He* died, to bring life to others.

As we have seen, Jonah is in some ways a type of Christ, but here he becomes also a type of a lost sinner seeking salvation. He tries to make a shelter for himself from the heat (of hell?), but his human efforts in building it are not sufficient.

Neither is anything in nature (even a miraculous plant) able to withstand or replace the shed blood of Christ, which condemns all man-made or nature-made works and alone can provide salvation — as God was now doing for the penitent Ninevites.

JONAH 4:8–9

> *And it came to pass, when the sun did arise, that God prepared a vehement east wind; and the sun beat upon the head of Jonah, that he fainted, and wished in himself to die, and said, It is better for me to die than to live.*
>
> *And God said to Jonah, Doest thou well to be angry for the gourd? And he said, I do well to be angry, even unto death.*

With the shade from the leaves of the gourd plant suddenly gone, Jonah again was subject to the searing heat of the desert. This was further aggravated by a *"vehement"* wind sent from the east by God. Any possible amelioration by westerly air flow from the Tigris plains or from the more distant Mediterranean was completely gone, and the heat blowing in from the desert was practically unbearable. The adjective "vehement" is used only this one time in the Bible, but it apparently conveys the nature of the dreaded east wind as somewhat quiet but extremely sultry and hot. Jonah almost had a sunstroke and was extremely faint.

Again he wanted to die, and so expressed himself to God. He somehow felt bitter about the withering of the gourd plant, which he had neither planted nor cultivated, but which he had enjoyed for a day and was now blaming God for its sudden demise.

"Why would God treat me this way?" he must have fumed. He had faithfully preached the message God wanted him to preach, but now he was on the verge of being viewed as a false prophet as well as a doomsayer, and he would probably be viewed with disdain even by his fellow countrymen back in Israel when he returned home. In fact, he would rather not have to return home at all. Better to die here in Assyria.

The Assyrians (remember that this "revival" took place only in Nineveh, not in Assyria as a whole) were still threatening Israel and the whole region. Nineveh was the largest city, but possibly not yet the capital, and there were other large cities in Assyria, as well as a powerful military machine on the frontiers. If Nineveh had been destroyed, that might have served as a warning to the whole Assyrian nation. But now, they were still a serious threat and would eventually conquer and enslave Jonah's people, just as he feared.

All of Jonah's fears suddenly boiled over and he let it all loose on the decayed remains of the gourd plant, which had now left him physically miserable in addition to his spiritual frustrations. He almost fainted in the heat, and wanted to die.

But God still cared about him and rebuked him gently, reminding him that he was venting his anger on a helpless plant that really could do nothing at all about his problems. He could at least have been thankful for the brief respite it *had* given him, recognizing that God had sent it in spite of his rebellious attitude about the conversion of the Ninevites. Their conversion itself could have been a source of rejoicing to him if he had tried harder to understand what God was doing in all this.

JONAH 4:10–11

> *Then said the LORD, Thou hast had pity on the gourd, for the which thou hast not laboured, neither madest it grow; which came up in a night, and perished in a night:*
>
> *And should I not spare Nineveh, that great city, wherein are more than sixscore thousand persons that cannot discern between their right hand and their left hand; and also much cattle?*

At this point, God taught Jonah the vital lesson he had been missing all along. His God of heaven was not only one of absolute holiness and perfect justice, who would *"by no means clear the guilty"* (Exod. 34:7), but also one who was *"keeping mercy for thousands, forgiving iniquity and transgression and sin"* (same verse, Exod. 34:7).

Jonah, courageous and zealous though he was, a true prophet who loved the Lord and the Lord's people, yet had been more solicitous of his own comfort as he watched for what he still hoped would be Nineveh's destruction than for the lives of the thousands of men, women, and (especially) innocent children who lived in that great city.

He was angry and irritated that the helpful shade of the gourd plant had been suddenly taken away, even blaming God for his discomfort and asking Him to take his life. No doubt he was well justified in his fear of the cruel Assyrians, but not all of them were irretrievable. In fact there were 120,000 who could not *"discern between their right hand and left hand,"* probably meaning very small children. And would Jonah like to see them destroyed with all their wicked leaders?

If Jonah had thought about the children, he might even have rationalized the situation by thinking that even they would be better off dead than being allowed to grow up into monsters like the others. But that clearly was not God's reasoning. Although most children raised in ungodly environments will, indeed, develop into ungodly men and women, it does not have to be so. We are told in the New Testament that Jesus Christ is *"the true Light, which lighteth every man that cometh into the world "* (John 1:9). There is much evidence of God in nature (Ps. 19:1; Rom. 1:20) and in the human heart (Rom. 2:14–15), and *"the eyes of the LORD run to and fro throughout the whole earth, to shew himself strong in the behalf of them whose heart is perfect toward him"* (2 Chron. 16:9).

That there is at least the possibility that even the worst of men can be converted to God had just been demonstrated to Jonah by the surprising Ninevite revival, and surely the children of these converts should have the same opportunity. If Jonah found it too difficult to forgive the adult Assyrians for their past atrocities, he could at least understand that their still-innocent children deserved a chance.

God also was concerned about even the cattle, of all things! In the complex of cities collectively called Nineveh, there were extensive open areas for pasturage, and it would be natural to expect that the large population (corresponding to 120,000 toddling children) would need large flocks of cattle (the term includes sheep and goats as well as cows) for food and clothing, and these would presumably also be killed in any kind of destructive calamity which God might have visited upon Nineveh.

It really is not surprising that God cares about His animal creation. After all, He did create them, and we have to believe He has a purpose for everything He has created. The great monologue of God in the Book of Job (chapters 38–41) is very largely about His providential care of His animal creatures, and there are numerous other biblical passages to the same effect. The Lord Jesus Christ taught that not even a sparrow shall *fall on the ground without your Father*" (Matt. 10:29).

And that's where Jonah ended his record. If some later scribe had written the book, as skeptics and liberals believe, that writer would certainly have felt it necessary to draw some moral or to tell what happened to Jonah afterwards or something. But the

Holy Spirit, through Jonah, chose to end it abruptly with this seemingly incidental mention of cattle.

Jonah, the real writer, and the Spirit of God guiding his writing, obviously felt that all the purposes of the account had been fulfilled with what had been written, and did not need any further exposition to distract the reader. But there are important applications that we today can see in this remarkable book, and some of these will be discussed in the next (and last) chapter.

EIGHT

JONAH AND THE TWENTY-FIRST CENTURY

The Book of Jonah was probably written no earlier than around 790 B.C., early in the reign of King Jeroboam II of Israel, although there has been much discussion about this. It was obviously written before the conquest and deportation of Israel into Assyria about 702 B.C., but after Assyria had become a great power and a serious threat to Israel. It does seem that the revival in Nineveh when Jonah preached there could not have lasted more than a generation. In any case, this was more than 25 centuries before our times today.

Yet its message has real significance for us here in the 21st century A.D. Many theologians, even those who deny its historicity, have agreed that its original purpose was to rebuke Jewish hyper-nationalism, showing that God had a deep concern for the Gentiles (even the most hated of all nations, the Assyrians), as well as for His chosen nation Israel.

The nations of Christendom, especially we here in America, undoubtedly need *that* message today as much as did ancient Israel. Patriotism is a virtue, but not "jingoism" or any form of racism.

Christians in particular know that *"God so loved the world"* (John 3:16) and that the Great Commission left by Christ commanded us *"that repentance and remission of sins should be preached in his name among all nations"* (Luke 24:47). We also realize that there will be people in heaven *"of all nations, and kindreds, and peoples, and tongues"* (Rev. 7:9). This was already a truth repeatedly emphasized by God to His elect nation Israel (Jonah should have remembered this) as in the great prophetic psalm of the future crucifixion of Messiah. There David had written by divine inspiration: *"All the ends of the world shall remember and turn unto the LORD: and all the kindreds of the nations shall worship before thee"* (Ps. 22:27).

Thus, one of the modern applications of the Book of Jonah is its missionary message. Jonah was sent by God to Nineveh, but we Christians have been sent into all the world to *"preach the gospel to every creature"* (Mark 16:15). If Jonah's experience can be considered a symbolic parallel, we could infer that those nations or individuals who oppose or ignore God's missionary command are thereby placing themselves in danger of some form of divine chastisement. God *does* want the gospel preached to all nations!

Our failure to do this effectively may well be one reason why Christ has not yet returned as He promised. Remember He said that *"the gospel must first be published among all nations"*

(Mark 13:10) and *"ye shall be witnesses unto me . . . unto the uttermost part of the earth"* (Acts 1:8).

In fact, the Bible says that during a coming time of tribulation, when it may well have become a capital crime to preach the gospel, God goes so far as to send an angel to do it, thereby emphasizing its importance. John says that, in his vision of this fearful time to come, *"I saw another angel fly in the midst of heaven, having the everlasting gospel to preach unto them that dwell on the earth, and to every nation, and kindred, and tongue, and people"* (Rev. 14:6).

Perhaps Jonah's message and experience can help in stressing the urgency of getting the gospel out in these latter days.

As already mentioned, Jonah himself can be considered a type of Christ and His saving power. He was willing to die in the violent storm waters in order to still the waters and save the lives of the mariners on the ship that were helping him flee from God's will. They were not even his friends but simply pagan sailors, yet he was willing to die — in fact *did* die — that their lives could be spared. Does not that act of self-sacrifice remind us of Romans 5:6–8? *"For when we were yet without strength, in due time Christ died for the ungodly. For scarcely for a righteous man will one die: yet peradventure for a good man some would even dare to die. But God commendeth his love toward us, in that, while we were yet sinners, Christ died for us."*

It is not wise to press biblical typology too far, as some have done. In Jonah's case, however, Christ himself confirmed that Jonah had indeed been a unique type of the coming Savior, when He said, *"For as Jonas was three days and three nights in the whale's belly; so shall the Son of man be three days and three nights in the heart of the earth"* (Matt. 12:40). In fact, Jonah was the only one of the prophets whom Jesus compared to himself. Jesus may well have visited Jonah's hometown, which was a short distance from Nazareth and was the traditional site of Jonah's tomb.

Further strengthening the typology, Jonah not only died for others, but descended into sheol (or hades, or hell), just as Christ did. Others have returned from death (and presumably sheol) just as Jonah did (e.g., Lazarus), but only Jonah had died to save others, as Christ did.

But Christ not only died for sinners; on the third day He rose again for their justification before God (Rom. 4:25). Jonah also rose on the third day to carry out His God-given mission.

The evidence for the bodily resurrection of the Lord Jesus Christ is so overwhelming that there would never have been Christianity without it. This is not the place to rehearse that body of evidence, but many, many books and articles have been published that do just that. Any open-minded person willing to look at the evidence is sure to conclude that the Lord Jesus *did* defeat death and therefore can save eternally all who put their trust in Him. *"I am he that liveth, and was dead,"* He said, *"and, behold; I am alive for evermore, Amen; and have the keys of hell and death"* (Rev. 1:18).

And, of course, this message of the substitutionary death and victorious resurrection of Christ complements perfectly the other message of Jonah, the missionary message. The saving gospel of Christ depends altogether on His resurrection, and *that* is the message that the missionary must carry, in addition to a warning of judgment to come if the gospel is refused.

The reality of hell is also a message that Jonah can help drive home. That doctrine is widely rejected and even ridiculed today, but Jonah, like Christ, was *there*! He came back to tell about it, but most people whose souls go there when their bodies die will never leave until the time of the second resurrection. At that time, as John reported from his vision, *"death and hell delivered up the dead which were in them"* (Rev. 20:13). However, this will be *"the resurrection of damnation"* about which Christ warned (John 5:29), for then they will be *"judged every man according to their works"* and — since no man can be saved by his works — all the inhabitants of that interim hell will be condemned: *"And whosoever was not found written in the book of life was cast into the lake of fire"* (Rev. 20:15), which is the ultimate hell, the eternal prison of lost souls.

There may be still another application of the Book of Jonah to the modern world situation, though this idea is equivocal at best, and may change with future developments. There does seem to be a sort of continuity between ancient Assyria and the nations that now occupy the lands of that region. The second half of the 20th century was a time of surprising awakening of practically all the lands and peoples of the Bible, so that the whole world is now occupied and concerned with events in that region. With the exception of the returned and reactivated nation of Israel (now largely humanistic, but with a very vocal Orthodox minority), that whole area is now almost wholly composed of Moslem nations dominated by the religion of Islam.

There has been much internal warfare, migration, and mixing among these Moslem nations, but practically all are enemies of Israel and violently opposed to having the revived nation of Israel in their midst. Some of these nations (e.g., Egypt) were originally Hamitic nations, but have been largely taken over by the Semitic Arabs. The latter mostly claim descent from Abraham through Ishmael or, to some extent, the sons of Keturah, Abraham's second wife. However, the term itself (Arab or Arabian) is never mentioned in the Bible before I Kings 10:15, during the time of King Solomon. In fact, the Tigris-Euphrates region, so long the homeland of Assyria and Babylonia, is also now largely Arabic.

The Arabian peninsula is vast, and many of the early tribes settled there, some developing into important kingdoms. With the coming of Islam, however, which had its origins in Arabia, great changes have taken place, and there is a measure of uncertainty about the early history of most of the modern nations in the Middle East.

As mentioned previously, both Assyria and Babylonia did exist in one form or another ever since the dispersion at Babel, and they were enemies all that time, with first one and then the other dominating. First Asshur and then Nineveh were capitals of Assyria, while Babylon (originally Babel) has usually been the capital of the Babylonian empire.

Assyria's final defeat came in 609 B.C., at the hands of a confederation headed by the Babylonians, with help from the Medes and Scythians (Nineveh itself was destroyed in 612 B.C.).

Babylon then became the greatest world empire for a time, until both the city and the empire were conquered by the Persian empire under Cyrus in 539 B.C.

In the time of Jonah, Assyria was still the dominant world empire, with Nineveh its greatest city.

These ancient empires — Babylonia and Assyria, as well as certain others are all mostly now part of present-day Iraq. The capital of Iraq, Baghdad, is very close to the ruins of Babylon, and Mosul, one of its chief cities, is just across the Tigris River from the ruins of Nineveh.

However, the present population of Iraq is believed to be mostly composed of Arabs. Descendants of the ancient Assyrians and Babylonians (to the extent they can be identified as such, since many have been assimilated over the centuries into other ethnic groups) are in small isolated pockets, many considering themselves Christian.

In a sense, therefore, modern Iraq is the successor to the ancient Assyro-Babylonian Empire(s), and its people are strongly tied to the great Moslem "empire," which originated in Saudi Arabia. The modern "king" of Iraq (as of 2003) has been a man named Saddam Hussein, whose control of the nation was just as strong and whose cruelty toward enemies just as notorious as those of any ancient Assyrian king. He was believed to have been developing weapons of mass destruction (biological, chemical, nuclear) which were an immediate lethal threat to all the world, especially Israel and America.

Saddam Hussein was — like the vast majority of people in the nations of the Middle East — a Moslem. Although his personal commitment to the tenets of Islam was said to be equivocal, he was also said to fancy himself as the prospective leader and spokesman of the whole Moslem world. He also fancied himself as the political successor to King Nebuchadnezzar of Babylonia and embarked on a serious attempt to rebuild the ancient city of Babylon, with the possible goal of making it the ultimate world capital.

Our own nation defeated Iraq in the so-called "Gulf War" of 1991, but Saddam seemed later to pose a greater danger than ever, and President George W. Bush, embarked with a pre-emptive war that would remove that danger. Whether this would actually happen was not known at the time of writing; and this writer does not profess to be a prophet.

Jonah *was* a prophet, however, and *his* prophecy proved invalid at that time, although Nineveh *was* destroyed over a century later, when the Assyrian repentance turned out to be superficial and temporary. At the same time, God's willingness to defer the destruction for a much longer time than the threatened 40 days is well worth noting.

Jonah was very fearful of what the unspeakable Assyrians would do to Israel and its people if God did not immediately fulfill His threat of catastrophic judgment on them. But he *did* finally obey God and preach to them. And, amazingly, they did repent and turn to God for at least a season.

In the meantime, Israel was spared an Assyrian invasion and conquest for another 65 years or so, very likely because of this revival in Nineveh. God also gave Israel ample time to repent, not only at the preaching of Jonah, but also that of Hosea and Amos. Instead they grew more rebellious and apostate than ever, until finally *"the LORD was very angry with Israel, and removed them out of his sight"* (2 Kings 17:18). And God *did* use the Assyrians for this purpose, as Jonah had feared.

If it is legitimate to use the story of Jonah and Nineveh as a teaching parallel to the present world situation, remembering that modern Iraq and its rulers have been anti-Christian in the extreme, as well as a potential deadly danger to America and the whole non-Moslem world, then perhaps God's commands to Jonah should be considered before we try to carry out our own plans for Iraq's future.

This should not be an action undertaken in deference to the U.N., however, because any admission that that body has jurisdiction over what action we take would be a tacit admission of allegiance to a world government controlled by humanistic (or worse) standards — in effect a vote for Antichrist.

But another way would be to first undertake a preaching ministry to the people of Iraq, like that of Jonah to Nineveh. And not just to Iraq, but to Moslems everywhere, for they all need to repent and turn to the true God. There may not be much time left to do this; even Moslems believe that Jesus is returning soon.

But they do not believe that Jesus was God incarnate or that He died for their sins, nor that He was buried, nor that He defeated death and rose again — and that's the very heart of His saving gospel (1 Cor. 15:1–4). Therefore, whether they believe in hell or not (and they do!), they are lost, like the Ninevites, and will spend eternity there away from the true God who created them. (Allah, of course, is a false god, the fallen angel who led Mohammed to write in the Koran that Christ was *not* the Son of God, and did *not* die and rise again.)

What is needed desperately is for the Christian community to deluge Iraq and other Moslem nations with the true gospel, by radio, books, and internet, as well as traditional personal missionaries. We deluged Iraq with political and military leaflets. How about using carefully designed Christian leaflets or tracts instead? Moslems already believe in creation and the Second Coming, and in parts of both Old and New Testaments. If they (especially their leaders) could somehow be helped to see and believe the truth about Christ and salvation, that would surely be better then either attacking potential enemies first or waiting for them to destroy us.

Undoubtedly the immediate reaction to such a suggestion will be that such an idea is absurd and impossible. Also, of course, most people in so-called Christendom would say that Moslems, Jews, and even pagans, can be saved by their own religion: it is religiously and politically incorrect to teach that one must accept Christ to be saved. Besides, the whole scenario is impossible.

But that is not what the Lord Jesus Christ said: *"I am the way,"* He said, *"no man cometh unto the Father, but by me"* (John 14:6). And He also insisted that *"with God all things are possible"* (Matt. 19:26).

What could seem less possible than a great and wicked city such as Nineveh suddenly turning to God? Yet it happened at the reluctant preaching of Jonah! And it happened after he had spent three days in the belly of a whale.

The Christian gospel is so clearly superior to the message of Islam — a living Savior instead of a dead prophet, a gracious God of love instead of a counterfeit god who instructs his followers to kill Jews and Christians (this command appears often in the Koran), a gospel that assures salvation to all who believe instead of a message that assures salvation (in a very sensual "paradise") only to those who die as martyrs for Allah — that a loving and intelligent witness concerning it ought surely to be convincing, especially if repeated often and supported by much prayer. Isn't it worth a try?

Probably the most "impossible" aspect of this concept, however, is not the mass winning of Moslems, but the massive cooperation of Christians in agreeing to carry out such a project.

Well, at least this is a possible message from Jonah to us in the 21st century, based on his remarkable journey from Israel to Nineveh, plus the amazing response to his message there in Nineveh some 2,700 years ago.

One of the mounds covering the ruins of ancient Nineveh today is called "Nebi Yunis," meaning "Prophet Jonah." There is no certainty that Jonah is actually buried there, of course. But the very persistence of his name there where proud Nineveh once thrived is a testimony today in that heart of the Moslem world (in Iraq, where for years the caliph of Baghdad was accepted as "king" of all Moslems) that faith in the true God of heaven once blanketed the greatest and arguably the most wicked city in the world of that time.

If it happened once, it could happen again. The same God of heaven still reigns.

OTHER BOOKS BY HENRY MORRIS

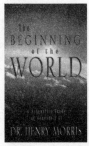

The Beginning of the World

Dr. Henry Morris gives a thorough explanation of the first 11 chapters of Genesis, the most contested chapters in the Bible. He shares his scientific insight and understanding in a format that can also be used for Bible studies.
Science and Faith
0-89051-162-4 • 184 pages • Paperback • $9.99

The Bible Has the Answer

Dr. Henry M. Morris & Martin E. Clark
How do we know the Bible is true? How will we spend eternity? Here is a complete resource to these and other tough questions facing every individual today.
Apologetics
0-89051-018-0 • 394 pages • Paperback • $11.99

Biblical Basis for Modern Science

Here is the most detailed analysis of all aspects of creation/evolution in one volume for the layperson. Includes illustrations, charts, tables, and appendixes and contains expositions of 12 major scientific disciplines, with all important Bible passages dealing with each.
Science & Faith
0-89051-369-4 • 475 pages • Paperback • $14.99

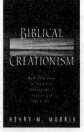

Biblical Creationism

This unique book discusses every passage in the Bible that deals with creation or the Flood. Dr. Morris shows that creation is taught not only in Genesis, but also throughout the whole Bible. Easy to understand and invaluable for all serious Bible students.
Science & Faith
0-89051-293-0 • 280 pages • Paperback • $12.99

Christian Education for the Real World

Dr. Henry Morris has developed a thoroughly biblical approach to education in the world today, based on over 50 years of experience in teaching and educational administration.
Education
0-89051-160-8 • 296 pages • Paperback • $10.99

Creation and the Second Coming

In this book, renowned creation scientist and theologian Dr. Henry Morris goes back to the beginning to unveil the details and events of our future. He begins the prophetic countdown at creation and reveals many fresh insights into Scripture.
Theology
0-89051-163-2 • 194 pages • Paperback • $10.99

Available at Christian bookstores nationwide